THE
BATTLE
F·O·R T·H·E
RESURRECTION

THE BATTLE

FOR THE

RESURRECTION

NORMAN L. GEISLER

THOMAS NELSON PUBLISHERS
Nashville

Published in Nashville, Tennessee, by Thomas Nelson, Inc. and distributed in Canada by Lawson Falle, Ltd., Cambridge, Ontario.

Printed in the United States of America.

Scripture quotations are from THE NEW KING JAMES VERSION of the Bible, copyright © 1979, 1980, 1982, Thomas Nelson, Inc., Publishers; the Revised Standard Version of the Bible, copyrighted 1946, 1952, © 1971, 1973; and The Holy Bible: New International Version, copyright 1978 by the New York International Bible Society; used by permission of Zondervan Bible Publishers

Library of Congress Cataloging-in-Publication Data

Geisler, Norman L
    The battle for the resurrection / by Norman L. Geisler.
      p   cm
    Includes bibliographical references.
    ISBN 0-8407-3035-7
    1. Jesus Christ—Resurrection   2. Jesus Christ—Historicity
    3. Jesus Christ—Person and offices.   I. Title.
    BT481.G45   1989   89–39083
    232.9'7—dc20   CIP

2 3 4 5 6 7 8 9 10 — 95 94 93 92 91 90

This book is gratefully dedicated to Dr. Robert Culver, long-time professor of theology at Trinity Evangelical Divinity School, who first brought this issue to my attention and from whose keen theological insight on the resurrection I have greatly profited.

Other Books by Norman L. Geisler

Contents

Acknowledgments

I am grateful to Dr. Robert Culver, Dr. William Craig, Jeffrey Donley, William Watkins, Samuel Kostreva III, Douglas Van Gordon, and Thomas Howe for reading this manuscript and making many helpful suggestions for improvement. Whatever imperfections remain, this book is certainly much better as a result of their suggestions.

Foreword

$\mathbf{D}$r. Geisler's timely book is accurately entitled *The Battle for the Resurrection,* but it also points to deeper doctrinal problems which have begun to surface in present-day evangelicalism.

Jesus is specifically the only Savior. He is our present Great High Priest, the only Mediator between God and man, Himself man, Christ Jesus (1 Tim. 2:5). The Bible teaches and the church creeds affirm that Jesus is forever more bone of our bone, partaker of our flesh and blood. He arose glorified from the dead in the body laid in the grave, the material, physical vessel of His humanity to which the second person of the Godhead is united for eternity. He continues to be a local physical being as to His manhood, ascended to heaven where He lives forever with the Father and the Holy Ghost and reigns until His enemies are made the footstool of His feet. Then He will come again, the very same Jesus, in the very same body.

Jesus did not, therefore, show up in Oklahoma recently, 900 feet tall, for the man of Nazareth, body and spirit, presently dwells in heaven. Most Christians believe that His seat at our communion tables is vacant, though they believe He is *spiritually* present in (1) Christians at the Lord's Table, (2) the elements of the Table, and (3) the pastor's sermon (as the Word of God).

One of the earliest creeds summarizes the relevant scripture teaching this way: He "suffered in the flesh [*en sarki*]; and rose again; and went up into heaven in the same body [*en auto somati*] . . . is coming in the same body [*en auto somati*] in glory" (*Second Creed of Epiphanius,* A.D. 374). It is easy to see that for this church father, body and flesh refer to the same.

Among the very first errors of doctrine in the Christian church were denials of the Lord's humanity.[1] That, of course, is why this is one of the few specific heresies treated in the New Testament. Before John was dead, he wrote these strident sentences: "try the spirits . . . . Hereby know ye the Spirit of God: Every spirit that confesseth that Jesus Christ is come in [the] flesh is of God: and every spirit that confesseth not that Jesus Christ is come in the flesh is not of God . . . . They are of the world . . . (1 John 4:1-3, 5 KJV). "For many deceivers are entered into the world, who confess not that Jesus Christ is come [i.e., has come and still is] in the flesh. This is a deceiver and an antichrist" (2 John 7).[2]

Any theory therefore which claims that the glorified body of our Lord is not flesh, but is instead essentially immaterial and angel-like, is neither orthodox nor scriptural. And the judgment of scripture on those who proclaim such a view is very severe—they are "false prophets . . . are not of God . . . of the world . . . deceivers . . . antichrist." Nothing in this book will be nearly as severe a judgment as these scriptural pronouncements.

Influential liberal scholars for seventy-five years or more have been saying that, while the body of Christ arose, it was as a "spiritual body"—immaterial, not flesh—thereby, misinterpreting Paul's expression. Several professors of New Testament, fresh from their university courses at secular universities, have been passing off this palpable nonsense to students at our colleges as learned, up-to-date, fresh, biblical scholarship—even though it is as old as the heretics whose errors made the earliest Christian creeds necessary. I personally have discovered this perspective taught in two evangelical schools. The theological illiteracy of some, the timidity of others, and the apathy of still others rendered my correction of a truly perilous situation nearly impossible at those times. Dr. Geisler has some enlightening tales of his own to tell about his experiences in the battle for the resurrection.

Now even some evangelical professors have refined the notion and subtly passed it off to the doctrinally illiterate as evangelical scholarship. This disguised liberalism may please some of the devotees of what goes today for biblical theology but it won't please anyone concerned about "the whole counsel of God."

Warren Wiersbe writes that serious reading is not a very popular way of spending spare time nowadays. How true! Perhaps that explains why responsible people at our Bible colleges and seminaries grant tenure to faculty members whose books plainly teach that the resurrection body of Jesus was essentially immaterial, non-fleshly and invisible; that he now is without human flesh in heaven and shall never again be seen in the flesh, and that, according to at least one evangelical professor, we receive our resurrection bodies at death (while our physical bodies are still in their graves!). (This is the view given great currency thirty-five years ago by Emil Brunner's book, *Eternal Hope*.) I think there is no other way to explain how superiors in administration, orthodox colleagues, and others act consistently to approve men holding these doctrinal aberrations from initial recommendation through committee, full faculty executive session, and even through denominational protocol. I certainly hope I am correct that not one of these many good people involved really knew exactly what these professors taught nor, if they did, understood the significance of it.

How can this be?

I think I know; at least I have a theory with respect to the denomination wherein I presently serve. In the first place, the Evangelical Free Church has never had a well-placed theological teacher to impart unity and coherence to its belief system—at least not for the last several decades. There has been great tolerance for variety—and not a little pride in it in a few quarters. "Believers only but all believers" remains a current ecclesiastical slogan, even though it suggests a doctrinal inclusiveness the early denomination's leaders did not really mean by it when it was first employed. This accords well with the pietistical spirit and independent, congregational polity of our group, within which I serve as a congregational pastor.

In the second place, though our seminary at first had a more or less firm commitment to the conservative theology of such respected schools as Moody Bible Institute, in recent decades the seminary has drawn in a mixed variety of theologies in an explosively expanded faculty and student body. There were then and still are few firm doctrinal commitments, except for an emphasis on plenary-verbal inspiration of the Bible—infallibility and inerrancy—and the seminary has always had a brief and not very extensive orthodox statement of faith which was adopted by the denomination when it achieved its present form and founded the school then known as Trinity Seminary and now known as Trinity Evangelical Divinity School. Yet theological pluralism, thought to be a strength, has great perils if uncontrolled by well-understood limits.

Doctrinal breadth and depth was lost in the late 1960's. Ordination councils, district ministerial boards, and congregations know what the young candidates believe only when they stand for examination—and then only if the questioners are sufficiently *concerned and* well informed to ask the right questions.

Piestistic and baptistic orthodox Christians tend to suppose their history of commitment to pure biblical faith is sufficient to protect themselves against theological error—or let us call it a doctrinal drift toward error. But history refutes them. I am not the first to question whether the particular pietistic denomination wherein I serve has firm enough roots in a sound system of theology to resist subtle inroads of misbelief and unbelief. In October 1960, *Bibliotheca Sacra,* the journal of Dallas Theological Seminary, published a review by G. W. Dollar of the book *Diamond Jubilee Story of the Evangelical*

Free Church of America, written by H. W. Norton, Olai Urang, R. A. Thompson, and Mel Larson. After kind, appreciative remarks, Mr. Dollar wrote:

> This reviewer noticed only one defect. Little reference was made to the danger of inroads of liberalism and neoorthodoxy to this church and whether there is *proper defence against such dangerous enemies when they appear* [emphasis added]. The Reformed tradition has been an obstacle to liberal views—but many institutions with informed circles have become soft toward liberalizing views and are now in the middle of the road. Will it happen to the Evangelical Free Church?[3]

There is a third factor: Some of the seminary's faculty (as alas is common in many other theological schools today) have graduate university training (secular, religious, or antireligious) for their doctorates but little or no study at a sound theological school with a standard curriculum of preparation for the pastoral ministry. So they may be quite thoroughly uninformed, misinformed, or even strongly prejudiced against systematic doctrinal study and necessary, careful, theological distinctions. For some, such important standard theological terms as *orthodoxy, dogmatics, apologetics* and the like are bad words. They know and love their specialties and put on their best performances for their professional peers.

In such a setting, theological acuity is not deemed important enough to think about very often and apparently not ever worth doing anything about. I can painfully report that this is so from experience in that setting. For a faculty member like me occasionally to be insistent on points of doctrine in examining prospects for teaching positions was not the way for me to gain approval among my peers and superiors. It took energy and fortitude to oppose some favored candidate, and I for one did not always have spunk enough to do so. One tires of controversy.

There is another factor more important than anything else, I think, in explaining how such a glaring doctrinal error slipped by unnoticed. A large section of the American evangelical church is almost hopelessly unconcerned theologically, except for well-worn shibboleths (which I hardly dare to mention) and cherished sectarian distinctives. Put another way, "The ethos of our church is pietistical and not theological." The pastor of one of the largest Free churches put it to me in those very words recently just before announcing his move to a different denomination. A variation of the same was put to me by the dean of faculty when I, a newcomer, assumed my duties at the seminary in September, 1951: "Out in the churches they will not ask what you are teaching here but 'Is the school having revival?'" The revival mood has passed. The lack of a sufficient theology remains. We are suffering from generations of inattention to systematic doctrinal instruction both in the lecture hall and in the pulpit.

About thirty years or more ago a small Baptist association, which had thought "the Bible, the whole Bible, and nothing but the Bible" was enough of a creed, went through a less painful form of this problem. One of their seminary's rising young teachers, a Ph.D named Bernard Ramm, wrote a series of articles advocating that even Baptists need some fairly complete statement of doctrine binding on ministers and schools. At the time, I was a Wheaton College professor and part-time pastor of one of their churches. I welcomed Dr. Ramm's faithful efforts. Much earlier, the Brethren (German Baptist, Dunker) denomination in which I grew up went through a similar painful trial, endemic among pietistic, independent Protestants. Accompanied by bitter controversy, agonizing schism, and permanent wounds, the Brethren had to adopt a clear, brief statement of faith for "the Brethren Ministry" and a much longer one (too long and too detailed on some nonessentials) for the college and seminary.

Now it is the turn of the Evangelical Free Church of America and their seminary, Trinity Evangelical Divinity School. It is going to be interesting to see what they will do about doctrinal laxity. They must both account for what they appear to have blundered somewhat innocently into and provide better insurance against doctrinal compromise for the future. Let us pray that the people responsible read *The Battle for the*

Resurrection, and discern the theological and doctrinal aberrations of those scattered in their ranks, and take a firm stand for orthodoxy.

Dr. Robert D. Culver
Long-time Professor of Theology
Trinity Evangelical Divinity School
Deerfield, Illinois

Error, indeed, is never set forth in its naked deformity, lest, being thus exposed, it should at once be detected. But it is craftily decked out in an attractive dress, so as by its outward form, to make it appear to the inexperienced . . . more true than truth itself———Irenaeus, *Against Heresies*, 1.2

Introduction

There is a trojan horse inside the evangelical camp. A new battle has broken out, and the enemy is on the inside, not the outside. In fact, the enemy has secretly placed dynamite at the evangelical foundation which supports the whole superstructure of Christian truth. Alarming? Yes, but true. Who is the enemy, and what is the evangelical foundation of truth?

The answer emerges from recent significant actions by some evangelical denominations. For example, one of the largest Protestant denominations in the world retains on the faculty of its school a professor who has denied in print that Jesus rose from the tomb in a literal, physical body. He contends

> Paul was convinced that the Christ who appeared to him belonged to another order of existence than the Christ the disciples had known in the flesh. *The risen Christ has not a physical but a spiritual body* (emphasis mine).

A smaller influential denomination that sponsors a well-known evangelical seminary in America has just pronounced orthodox a professor who denies what the Apostle's Creed affirms: "I believe . . . in the resurrection of the body [flesh]." He wrote of Christ:

This suggests that after his resurrection *his essential state was one of invisibility and immateriality.*

It will be spiritual also in that it is . . . *neither fleshly nor fleshy.*

From this point of view the new body is qualitatively and *numerically distinct* from the old body (emphases mine).

These developments signal a new and crucial battle inside the evangelical church—the battle for the resurrection. Fighting for the resurrection is not new; fighting for it inside evangelical circles is. Once it was only liberals who denied the physical, material resurrection; now some evangelicals have joined them. Traditionally, the historicity of the resurrection was denied; now it is the materiality of the resurrection body that is denied.

Suppose you were in Jesus' tomb on that first Easter morning. What would you have seen? Jesus' dead body literally come to life and leave the tomb? No. According to this new departure from orthodoxy, you simply would have witnessed Jesus' body vanish before your eyes! In short, you would have observed the annihilation of His material body, not its resurrection.

The implications of this new doctrinal departure are far reaching. They threaten the very foundation of our evangelical faith. The Bible declares that the resurrection is the very heart of the gospel (1 Cor. 15:1-3) and is even a condition of salvation (Rom. 10:9). Thus, to tamper with this foundation of faith is to undermine the whole superstructure of Christian truth.

This book is an attempt to sound the trumpet of concern about this current trend in evangelical doctrine. It reveals alarming information about the latest attempts to redefine historic biblical truths to suit contemporary inclinations. It is an earnest plea to alert the body of Christ to one of the most significant doctrinal deviations of our time—one that hits at the very essence of the Christian faith.

The Trojan horse is within and the dynamite has been placed. The battle for the resurrection has begun!

1

The Battle for the Resurrection

First it was the battle for the Bible; now it is the battle for the resurrection. First the question was whether we can trust what the Bible says about itself; now the question is whether we can trust what the Bible says about the resurrection. First it was whether inspiration covered only spiritual matters but not historical and scientific statements. Now it is whether the resurrection body is only spiritual (that is, immaterial) or whether it is material, and historically and empirically observable.

Satan's strategy does not change. He begins by casting doubt on God's Word. "Did God really say?" he questioned Eve. "Are you really sure it means that?" For generations Christians accepted the simple statements of the Bible about itself (the Written Word of God) and about Christ (the Living Word of God). The Devil's device, however, has been to challenge God's authority in both areas.

Then, if Satan is not successful in casting doubt on God's Word, he will find new ways to "spiritualize" away its literal truth. That is, if he cannot get people to doubt *that* the Bible is God's Word, he will get them to question *how* it is to be interpreted. Satan's double-barreled attack is on the inspiration *and* interpretation of the Bible. The first strategy worked with the theological liberals. The second strategy is aimed at evangelicals.

First Satan suggested "The Bible is true, but do not take it literally." Now he suggests, "Christ rose from the dead but not in a literal body." The Enemy of Christianity cannot accept the straight-forward, literal truth of Scripture, especially about itself. For if the Bible is literally true, then Satan is condemned (Gen. 3; Eph. 4). Satan is also doomed if Christ rose from the dead in a literal, physical body (Heb. 2:14; Col. 2:14). Therefore, one of Satan's most effective strategies down through the centuries has been to "spiritualize" or allegorize away the literal truth of Scripture.

The Battle for the Bible

The Bible clearly declares itself to be the Word of God (Matt. 5:17–18; John 10:35; 2 Tim. 3:16).[1] It also informs us that God cannot err (Heb. 6:18; Titus 1:2). If these two propositions are true, then the conclusion is inevitable: The Bible cannot err. If the Bible erred in anything it affirmed, then God would be mistaken. This is the uncompromisable truth at stake in the "battle for the Bible."[2]

The Bible Is the Word of God

Jesus referred to the Old Testament as the "Word of God" which "cannot be broken" (John 10:35). He said, "until heaven and earth disappear, not the smallest letter, not the least stroke of a pen, will by any means disappear from the Law until everything is accomplished" (Matt. 5:18 NIV). Paul added, "All Scripture is God-breathed . . ." (2 Tim. 3:16 NIV). It came "from the mouth of God" (Matt. 4:4 NIV). Although human authors recorded the messages, "prophecy never had its origin in the will of man, but men spoke from God as they were carried along by the Holy Spirit" (2 Peter 1:20 NIV).[3]

The religious leaders of Jesus' day were not content with the simple authority of the Word of God. They obscured its authority by their own speculations about and elaborations on the Old Testament. Hence, Jesus said to them, "you nullify the word of God by your tradition . . ." (Mark 7:13 NIV).

Jesus turned their attention to the written Word of God by affirming over and over again, "It is written . . . It is written . . . It is written . . ." (Matt. 4:4, 7, 10). This phrase occurs over ninety times in the New Testament. It is a strong indication of the divine authority of the written Word of God.

Stressing the unfailing nature of God's truth, the Apostle Paul referred to the Scriptures as "the word of God" (Rom. 9:6 RSV). The writer of Hebrews declared that "the word of God is living and active. Sharper than any double-edged sword, it penetrates even to dividing soul and spirit, joints and marrow; it judges the thoughts and attitudes of the heart" (Heb. 4:12 NIV). It is this powerful and simple Word that the apostle spoke of when he warned against "handling the word of God deceitfully" (2 Cor. 4:2 NKJV).

God Cannot Err

Another simple and unadulterated truth is that God cannot err. The Scriptures declare emphatically that "it is impossible for God to lie" (Heb. 6:18 NKJV). Paul speaks of the "God who cannot lie" (Titus 1:2 NKJV). God is truth (John. 14:6), and so is His Word. Jesus said to the Father, "Your word is truth" (John 17:17 NKJV). The psalmist exclaimed, "the entirety of Your word is truth, and every one of Your righteous judgments endures forever" (Ps. 119:160 NKJV).

The Bible Cannot Err

What is the battle for the Bible all about? Put in simple terms, it is this: God cannot err, so His Word cannot err. If the Bible is God's Word, and God cannot err, then it follows necessarily that the Bible cannot err. Let's state the issue in logical form:

1) The Bible is the Word of God.
2) God cannot err.
3) Therefore, the Bible cannot err.

Yes, God has spoken, and He has not stuttered. The God of truth has given us the Word of Truth, and it does not contain any untruth in it. The Bible is the unerring Word of God.[4] This is what the battle for the Bible is all about.

Of course, wherever God makes something clear, Satan denies it, or at least confuses it. Whenever God speaks with authority, the Devil tries to undermine it. "Did God really say that?" he sneers (Gen. 3:1).

This confusion often takes the following form: The Bible may be God's Word in some sense, but it is also human words. It had human authors, and "to err is human." Hence, we are to expect some errors in the Bible. So goes the argument.

In short, the clear and simple truth of God is confused by the lie of Satan, the master of lies (John 8:44).

Let's analyze what is wrong with this reasoning. A simple analogy will help. Consider equally faulty reasoning that parallels the divine/human authorship controversy above:

1) Jesus was a human being.
2) Human beings sin.
3) Therefore, Jesus sinned.

Any Bible student can readily see that this conclusion is not true, even if it follows a logical form. What do we *mean* by saying, "Jesus was a human being"? The Bible tells us that Jesus was "without sin" (Heb. 4:15 NKJV). He "had no sin" (2 Cor. 5:21 NIV). Jesus was "a lamb without blemish or defect" (1 Peter 1:19 NIV). As John said of Jesus, "he is pure" and "righteous" (1 John 3:3; 2:1 NIV). But if Jesus never sinned, then what is wrong with the above argument that Jesus is human and humans sin, therefore, Jesus sinned? Where does the logic go astray?

The mistake is to assume that Jesus is like any other human. Sure, mere human beings sin. But Jesus was not a *mere* human being. He was a *perfect* human being. Indeed, Jesus was not only human, but He was also God. Likewise, the Bible is not a mere human book. It is also the Word of God. Like Jesus, it is both divine and human. (Although Jesus is a divine Person, and the Bible is a divine book.) And just as Jesus was human but did not sin, even so the Bible is a human book but does not err. Both God's Living Word (Christ) and His Written Word (Scripture) are human but do not err. They are divine and cannot err. There can no more be an error in

God's Written Word than there can be a sin in God's Living Word. God cannot err, period. Of course, Jesus was sinless and the writers of Scripture were not. However, God preserved them from error when they wrote Scripture. So the end result is the same in the cases of Jesus and the Bible.

In short, the question in the "battle for the Bible" is this: Can God err? The answer is that if the Bible is God's Word and God cannot err, then it follows necessarily that the Bible cannot err. So to say there is even one error taught in the Bible is to mar the character of God. The battle for the Bible is a battle for the character of God. Can God be trusted to tell the truth, the whole truth, and nothing but the truth?

The Battle for the Resurrection

What, then, is the battle for the resurrection? Just as the simple truth about the Bible has been obscured by the teachings of men, likewise, the simple truth about the resurrection is now being confused by semantical subtlety.

The Bible teaches that Christ rose from the grave bodily. His body was a physical, material organism, just like any other human body. Therefore, it follows that Christ rose in a physical, material body (see Glossary). However, this simple truth is being confused by some who redefine clear terms and contend that Christ arose bodily; but not in a *material* body. Such a view is unorthodox and can be contrasted with the biblical view as follows:

ORTHODOX VIEW	UNORTHODOX VIEW
The Same Body	A Different Body
(Numerically Identical)	(Numerically Distinct)
A Material Body	An Immaterial Body
In the Flesh	Not in the Flesh
In History	Not in History
(In Space and Time)	(Not in Space and Time)

First of all, the Bible declares that the *same body* placed in Jesus' tomb on Good Friday emerged from it on Easter Sun-

day. The body placed there was a physical, material body
Hence, it follows that the risen body was also that same physical, material body.

Second, the resurrection body is described as a material
body. Jesus said it had "flesh and bones" (Luke 24:39). It
had the scars from His crucifixion on it (John 20:27) and even
ate physical food (Luke 24:42, 43). People saw Him with
their naked eyes and touched Him with their hands (Matt.
28:9).

Furthermore, Scripture informs us that Jesus came in the
"flesh" (John 1:14) and was resurrected in the same "flesh"
(see Luke 24:39; Acts 2:31). Doctrine which denies "that
Jesus Christ has come [and remains] in the flesh" is not of
God (1 John 4:2 NKJV). Yet this is precisely what some evangelicals are teaching today.

Moreover, the Bible declares that Christ arose "on the third
day" (1 Cor. 15:4 NIV). That is, it was a chronologically dat-
able event in history. It was not a supra–historical event beyond space and time. Rather, it was an empirical event in real
history.

By contrast, one scholar contends that:

> Because the life of the resurrected Lord involves the reality of
> the new creation, the resurrected Lord is in fact *not perceptible
> as one object among others in this world;* therefore, he could only
> be experienced and designated by an extraordinary mode of
> experience, the vision, and only in metaphorical language
> (emphasis mine).[5]

Another professor claims that "As a non-empirical event of
and with Jesus himself after his death, the resurrection is
per se trans-historical . . ." (emphasis mine).[6]

The Importance of the Bodily Resurrection

Few doctrines are more crucial to Christianity than the
bodily resurrection of Christ (see Chapter 2). It is at the very
heart of the gospel (1 Cor. 15:1–5). Without the resurrection
there is no salvation (Rom. 10:9), and the whole of Christianity crumbles if it is not true (1 Cor. 15:12–19). The Bible pro-
claims plainly that three days after His crucifixion, Jesus

permanently vacated His tomb. The angel said, "He is not here; for He is risen, as He said" (Matt. 28:6 NKJV).

Indeed, Jesus said over and over that He would die and rise again (John 2:19; Matt. 12:40; 17:9; 18:23). There are five different accounts showing that Jesus' prediction about His resurrection was fulfilled literally (Matt. 28; Mark 16; Luke 24; John 20–21; 1 Cor. 15). Jesus did rise bodily from the grave, and He left an empty tomb behind. The crucified body that was placed there on Good Friday left on Easter Sunday.

Three days after Jesus died and the tomb was found empty, He began appearing to His disciples in this same body, giving them "many convincing proofs" that he was alive for over forty days (Acts 1:3 NIV). Jesus made at least twelve separate appearances to a total of over 500 people (1 Cor. 15:6) covering a forty day period of time (see Chapter 8).

During Jesus' bodily resurrection appearances, the disciples saw Him, heard Him, touched Him, and witnessed Him eat on four occasions (Luke 24:30, 43; John 21:13; Acts 1:4). Jesus showed them His crucifixion scars (John 20:27) and said, "Touch me and see; a ghost does not have flesh and bones, as you see I have" (Luke 24:39 NIV). It is clear that Jesus rose in the same body in which He was crucified. He did not rise as a spirit, but in a real tangible, material body.

The resurrected Christ made such an indelible impression on the early disciples that it was the very core of their preaching (Acts 2, 4, 10, 17). Paul established the resurrection as a condition of salvation (Rom. 10:9), and declared that if Christ did not rise we are still in our sins and are of all people most miserable (1 Cor. 15:17–19). Indeed, if Christ did not rise from the grave in the same physical body that died, then death and Satan were not defeated, as the Scriptures triumphantly proclaim they were (Heb. 2:14; Col. 2:14).

The Nature of the Resurrection Body

The logic is clear: If Jesus rose bodily from the dead in the same body in which He died, and if this body was a physical, material body, then it follows that the resurrection body was a physical, material body. Let's examine the premises:

1) Jesus rose bodily from the grave in the same body in which He died.
2) The body in which Jesus died was a physical, material body.
3) Therefore, Jesus' resurrection body is a physical, material body.

Here again, nothing could be simpler: Jesus rose bodily, and a "body" is, as *Webster* says, "an organized physical substance . . . the material part or nature of a human being."[7] In fact, the Greek word for "body" *(soma)* always means a physical body when referring to an individual human being.[8] There are no exceptions to this usage in the New Testament. But if "body" always refers to a physical, material organism, and Christ rose bodily, then His resurrection must have been in a physical, material body.

The Resurrection Challenge

Like the battle for the Bible, the battle for the resurrection is about another fundamental doctrine. It is a battle over another attempt to confuse the simple truth of Scripture on a vital issue.

Those who deny the inerrancy of the Bible wish to limit its divine authority to "spiritual" matters. They deny inerrancy on historical and scientific issues.

Some are now contending that the resurrection body was only "spiritual" or immaterial. They deny that the resurrection was empirically observable or historically verifiable. This platonic (and gnostic) tendency to "spiritualize" or allegorize the literal truth of Scripture is not new. What is new is that those who claim to be evangelicals apply it to fundamental doctrines of the Christian faith, such as the inspiration of the Bible and the resurrection of Christ.

The bodily resurrection of Christ is an indispensable foundation of the Christian faith. No deviation on this doctrine should be tolerated within the ranks of orthodox Christianity. In spite of this, many evangelicals are now pronouncing orthodox the view that Jesus did not rise in the same material body of flesh in which He died. This denial of the historical biblical doctrine of the resurrection is a serious crisis at the very heart of the evangelical Christian faith.

THE BATTLE FOR THE RESURRECTION HAS BEGUN!

2

It Makes a Difference

What difference does it make whether or not Christ rose from the dead in the same physical body in which He died? The New Testament's answer to this question is unequivocal: Without Christ's bodily resurrection there is no salvation (Rom. 10:9–10; 1 Thess. 4:14). For He "was delivered over to death for our sins and was raised to life for our justification" (Rom. 4:25 NIV). The bodily resurrection of Christ is just as much a part of the gospel as is His death (1 Cor. 15:1–5).

The apostle Paul insisted that if Jesus did not rise bodily (physically, materially) from the dead, then: 1) Our faith is useless; 2) We are still in our sins; 3) Our departed loved ones are lost; 4) The apostles are false witnesses; 5) and we are to be pitied more than all men (1 Cor. 15:14–19).[1] This is a sobering list of consequences for denying the physical resurrection of Christ. In short, if Christ did not arise bodily from the tomb, Christianity is false, we cannot be saved, and there is no hope for our bodily immortality. For it is "Christ who has . . . brought life and immortality to light through the gospel" (2 Tim. 1:10 NKJV).

The Resurrection Body of Christ

Orthodox Christianity has always confessed two things about the resurrection body of Christ: it was the same physical body in which Jesus was crucified (see Chapter 4), and it was an immortal body. Both are important to a biblical view of the resurrection, but the former is the primary focus of this book.

The Historic Importance of the Physical Resurrection

In his classic, *History of Christian Doctrine*, evangelical theologian William G. T. Shedd noted that "the doctrine of the resurrection of the body was from the beginning a cardinal and striking tenet of the Christian Church."[2] Historically, the bodily resurrection has been taken to mean a physical, material body. Indeed, even some scholars who oppose this belief admit that "until the time of the Reformation the creeds of the West spoke only of the resurrection of the flesh *(sarkos anastasis; resurrectio carnis)*."[3]

Contemporary Affirmations of the Resurrection

When evangelical confessions or creeds state that "He [Christ] rose bodily from the dead" or "we believe in the bodily resurrection of all the dead,"[4] we instinctively understand this to mean *physical* body. Hence, it has seemed unnecessary to most evangelicals to add words like "material" or "physical" to the word "body" in this context. That is exactly what the words "bodily resurrection" mean. Some speak of "resurrection," not "physical resurrection," for the simple reason that as normally understood this phrase is redundant. And fewer still speak of a "material" body, since all physical bodies are material. *Webster* defines "body" as an "organized physical substance."[5] So to speak of a *physical* or *material* body is really redundant.

To speak of an immaterial body or a "spiritual corporeality"[6] is a contradiction of terms. As *Webster* notes, a body is "the material part of nature."[7] And the English word "spirit" by definition is something immaterial. Hence, an immaterial body would be an immaterial material, which is a contradiction in terms. Since it is redundant to speak of a physical body and contradictory to refer to an immaterial body, it is understandable that many evangelical creeds and confessions speak simply of the "resurrection of the body" (see Chapter 4).

Some unorthodox Christian teachers, like Origen, denied the material nature of Christ's human body.[8] First John was written to counteract a similar teaching that denied that "Jesus Christ has come in the flesh" (1 John 4:2 NKJV). When this same kind of error appeared later in church history, Christians used the even more explicit confession of the "resurrection of the *flesh*"[9] to describe the resurrection body (see Chapter 4). This emphasizes the fact that "body" means a material body. So, contrary to a current theological trend, to affirm that bodily resurrection means anything other than a physical, material body is illogical, unhistorical, and unorthodox.

The Importance of the Resurrection's Physical Nature

Does it really make any difference whether Jesus rose in a material body or in an immaterial one? Does it really matter whether He was raised in the flesh or merely in an angel-like body? As long as we believe that Christ's body mysteriously vanished from the tomb, isn't that enough?

Actually, the significance of the physical resurrection of Christ is far-reaching, and the implications of its denial are fundamental to orthodox Christianity. In fact, a denial of it affects our very salvation.

The Problem of Creation

God created a material world and pronounced it very good (Gen. 1:31).[10] Sin disrupted the world and brought decay and death (Gen. 2:17; Rom. 5:12). The whole of material creation was subjected to bondage because of man's sin (Rom. 8:18ff.). However, through redemption, decay and death will be reversed. For "creation itself will be liberated from its bondage to decay . . ." (v. 21 NIV).

Indeed, "the whole [material] creation has been groaning . . . as we wait eagerly for our adoption as sons, the redemption of our bodies" (vv. 22–23 NIV). That is, God will reverse the curse upon material creation by a material resurrection. Anything less than the resurrection of the material body would not restore God's perfect material creation, including mankind. Hence, an immaterial resurrection is contrary to God's creative purposes. Just as God will recreate the material universe (Rev. 21:1-4; 2 Peter 3:10-13) in redeeming the old one, even so He will reconstitute the material body in redeeming the one that died.

Anything short of a material recreation of the world and a material reconstruction of the body would spell failure for God's creative purpose. New Testament scholar Robert Gundry notes, "Anything less than that undercuts Paul's ultimate intention that redeemed man possess physical means of concrete activity for eternal service and worship of God in a restored creation."[11] So "to dematerialize resurrection, by any means, is to emasculate the sovereignty of God in both creative purpose and redemptive grace."[12]

The Problem of Salvation

There are serious *salvation* problems in denying the physical nature of the resurrection of Christ. As pointed out earlier, the New Testament teaches that belief in the bodily resurrection of Christ is a condition for salvation (Rom. 10:9, 10; 1 Thess. 4:14). It is part of the essence of the gospel itself (1 Cor. 15:1-5). But, as we shall see (in Chapter 6), the New Testament's understanding of "body" *(soma)* was of a literal, physical body. Hence, a denial of the physical, bodily resurrection of Christ undercuts the very gospel itself.

Without a physical resurrection there is no material continuity between the pre- and post-resurrection body. They would be two different bodies.[13] However, as Professor Gundry correctly observes: "A physical continuity is also needed. If a human spirit—a sort of third party—be the only connection between the mortal and resurrected bodies, the relationship of the two bodies to each other is extrinsic and to that degree unimpressive as a demonstration of Christ's victory over death."[14] In even stronger terms he concludes that "the resurrection of Christ was and the resurrection of Christians will be physical in nature."[15] Without a physical resurrection there is no ground for celebrating Christ's victory over physical death.

The Problem of the Incarnation

The denial of the material nature of the resurrection body is a serious *doctrinal* error. It is a kind of neodocetism. The docetics were a second century sect which denied that Jesus was truly human.[16] It taught that Jesus was really God but that He only appeared to be human. It denied that He had real human flesh.

A similar doctrinal deviation existed in the first century. John speaks to it when he warns against those who deny that "Jesus Christ has come in the *flesh*" (1 John 4:2 cf. 2 John 7 NIV, emphasis mine). In fact, when John said "has come" (in the perfect participle tense in Greek) he implies that Christ came in the flesh and still remains after His resurrection in the flesh.[17] This means that denying Christ had a material body either before or after His resurrection is false doctrine. This is exactly what the current post-resurrectional doceticism does. It denies that the one who came in the flesh was also raised in the flesh.[18]

Having human flesh is essential to the full humanity of Christ and is used repeatedly to describe it (John 1:14; 1 Tim. 3:16; 1 John 4:2; 2 John 7). If this is so, then unless Christ arose in the flesh, He was not raised fully human (1 Tim. 2:5). This is particularly acute, since Christ's ministry for our salvation did not end at the Cross. According to Hebrews, Christ "ever lives to make intercession" for us (Heb. 7:25 NKJV). Indeed, it is because Jesus was and is fully human that He is able to "sympathize with our weaknesses" in His high priestly ministry (Heb. 4:15 NKJV). Therefore, Christ's full resurrected humanity is necessary for our salvation. According to Scripture, human *flesh* was part of His full humanity. Unless Christ rose in the flesh, His full human nature was not restored, and He is not our divine/human mediator (1 Tim. 2:5).

The Problem of Human Immortality

Further, denying the physical resurrection causes a serious problem with Christian *immortality*. If Christ did not rise in the same physical, material body in which He was crucified, then we have no hope that we will be victorious over physical death either. It is only through the physical resurrection of Christ that the believer can triumphantly proclaim: "Where, O death, is your victory? Where, O death, is your sting?" (1 Cor. 15:55 NIV). It is only through the physical resurrection that Christ has "destroyed death and has brought life and immortality to light through the gospel" (2 Tim. 1:10 NIV). Paul told the Corinthians, "if Christ has not been raised . . . those also who have fallen asleep in Christ are lost" (1 Cor. 15:17, 18 NIV).

The Problem of Moral Deception

There is a serious *moral* problem of deception in denying the physical resurrection. No one can look squarely at the gospel record of Christ's post-resurrection appearances and deny that Jesus tried to convince the skeptical disciples that He had a real physical body. He said, "Look at my hands and my feet. It is I myself! Touch me and see; a ghost does not have flesh and bones, as you see I have" (Luke 24:39 NIV). He ate in their presence (vv. 41–43). He challenged Thomas: "Put your finger here; see my hands. Reach out your hand and put it into my side. Stop doubting and believe" (John 20:27 NIV).

Given the context of Jesus' claim and of the Jewish belief in the physical resurrection (see Acts 23:8; John 11:24), it is inescapable that Jesus intentionally persuaded His disciples to believe His resurrection on the basis of His appearances in the same material, fleshly body they had known for over three years and had laid in the tomb only days before. If Jesus' resurrection body was only an immaterial body, then Jesus was knowingly misleading his disciples. That is, He was intentionally leading them to believe what He knew was not true. In short, if Jesus' resurrection body was not a physical, material body, then He was lying.

The Problem of Verification

There is also an important *evidential* implication of denying a material resurrection body. If Christ did not rise in the same physical body that was placed in the tomb, then the resurrection loses its value as an evidential proof of His claim to be God (John 8:58; 10:30). The resurrection cannot verify Jesus' claim to be God unless He was resurrected in the body in which He was crucified. That body was a literal, physical body. Unless Jesus rose in a material body, there is no way to verify His resurrection. It loses its historically persuasive value.

The truth of Christianity is based on the bodily resurrection of Christ. Jesus offered His coming resurrection as a proof of His deity throughout His ministry (John 2:19-22; Matt. 12:38-40; John 10:18). In one passage He presented His resurrection as the unique evidence of who He was. Jesus said to those seeking a "sign,"

> But none will be given it except the sign of the prophet Jonah. For as Jonah was three days and three nights in the belly of a huge fish, so the Son of Man will be three days and three nights in the heart of the earth (Matt. 12:40 NIV).

The apostles considered His resurrection appearances as "many convincing proofs" (Acts 1:3 NIV). They used the fact of Christ's bodily resurrection as the basis of their argument for the claims of Christ over and over again (see Acts 2:22-36; 4:2, 10; 13:32-41; 17:1-4, 22-31). Paul concluded that God "has given proof . . . to all men by raising him from the dead" (Acts 17:31 NIV).

The physical continuity between the pre- and post-resurrection body of Christ is made repeatedly in apostolic preaching. Peter's first sermon declared that the Jews "put him to death by nailing *him* to the cross. But God raised *him* from the dead . . ." (Acts 2:23-24 NIV, emphasis mine). He adds, "he was not abandoned to the grave, nor did *his body* see decay. God has raised *this Jesus* to life, and we are witnesses of the fact" (vv. 31-32 NIV, emphasis mine). Paul is equally specific in making the connection between the actual body that was put in the grave and the one that was resurrected. He says, "they took *him* down from the tree and laid *him* in a tomb. But God raised *him* from the dead . . ." (Acts 13:29–31 NIV, emphasis mine).

Why is it so important to Christ's claim to deity that His resurrection body be the same physical body that was laid in the tomb? The answer is twofold.

First, this is the only way to know for sure that the resurrection occurred. The empty tomb in itself does not prove the resurrection of Christ any more than a missing body in a morgue proves someone has resurrected. Neither does an empty tomb plus a series of appearances prove the resurrection. The original body could have disappeared and the appearances could have been of someone else. But in a theistic context, where miracles are possible, an empty tomb plus appearances of the *same physical body,* once dead but now alive, are proof of a miraculous resurrection. Without this material identity between the pre- and post-resurrection body, the apologetic value of the resurrection is destroyed.

Second, unless Christ rose in a physical, material body the resurrection is unverifiable. There is no way to verify empirically that He was really resurrected unless He was resurrected in the same physical body in which He died and was buried. If the resurrected body was essentially immaterial and "angel-like,"[19] then there is no way to verify that the resurrection occurred. For a miraculous manifestation in an angel-like form does not prove a bodily resurrection. At best, such an angel-like manifestation only proves that there is a spirit with the power to "materialize" or reappear after it has departed from the body.

However, even angels who are pure spirits and never had been incarnated (Heb. 1:14) had the power to "materialize" (Gen. 18). The angels who appeared to Abraham miraculously assumed visible form (Gen. 18:8; 19:3). But this was not a proof that they possessed by nature physical bodies like ours. In fact, angels do not have physical bodies; they are spirits (Heb. 1:14; Luke 24:39; Matt. 22:30). Nor were their manifestations in physical continuity with a previous earthly body, as is the case with the resurrection body of Christ. The angelic manifestations were merely temporarily assumed forms for the purpose of communicating with human beings. To place Jesus' appearances in this category is to reduce his physical resurrection to an angelic manifestation. It is to downgrade resurrection into theophany (See Appendix B).

It is not only demeaning to the nature of the resurrection body of Christ to call it "angel-like," it is also destructive of its evidential value. There is a real difference between an angelic manifestation and a literal, physical body. A mere angelic "materialization" is not proof that the angel possesses a real physical body, as Christ's resurrection appearances were adduced to prove. An essentially immaterial resurrection "body" is no more proof of Christ's bodily resurrection than is an angelic manifestation a proof that an angel once died in a physical body and was resurrected. Resurrection in an immaterial body is no proof that Christ conquered death in His material body (1 Cor. 15:54–56). In brief, an immaterial resurrection body is evidentially not different from *no* resurrection body at all.

Make No Mistake

Any denial of the physical, bodily resurrection of Christ is critical. Denial by evangelicals is even more serious. This is particularly true when they use the traditional term "bodily resurrection" to affirm their view. "Bodily" resurrection has always meant that Jesus was resurrected in the same physical, material body in which He died.

In spite of the overwhelming biblical evidence that Christ arose in the same fleshly body in which He was crucified, some evangelicals are now claiming that He did not rise in the flesh but in an immaterial body. But a physical body is a material body. Hence, an immaterial physical body is impossible. Either Christ rose immortally in the same material body in which He lived before His death, or He did not rise at all. As the poet John Updike puts it,

Make no mistake; if He rose at all
   it was as His body,
if the cells' dissolution
   did not reverse,
   the molecules reknit,
   the amino acids rekindle,
the Church will fall.[20]

3

The Bible on the Resurrection

Evangelicals have always affirmed two basic things about the resurrection body of Christ: It is physical, and it is immortal. It is a body of flesh, and yet it is glorified flesh. That is, the post-resurrection body is as material as the pre-resurrection body, yet it is as immortal as the soul.

The Resurrection Body

It is a *soma* (physical body), but it is a spirit-dominated body *(soma pneumatikon)*, as Paul said in 1 Corinthians 15:44. These beliefs are firmly based in Holy Scripture and have been confessed consistently by the Christian Church through the centuries. This chapter provides a detailed biblical basis for the orthodox doctrine of the physical resurrection.

Its Physical Nature

To emphasize the physical, material nature of the resurrection body, orthodox Christians through the ages consistently have called it the resurrection of the "flesh" (see Chapter 4). Some evangelical confessions have been content with the word "body," since its ordinary meaning implies that which is material and physical. The two words are used interchangeably.

Belief in the physical resurrection is based on the fact that at His resurrection, Jesus permanently vacated the tomb in the same physical body in which He had been crucified. Jesus' resurrection body had crucifixion scars, could be seen and handled, and could even eat food. Even Jesus said it was a body of "flesh [*sarx*] and bones" (Luke 24:39 NKJV). This same word "flesh" *(sarx)* is used to describe His incarnation into a material human body (John 1:14). The apostle John considered denial of it to be false teaching (1 John 4:2; 2 John 7).

Some have suggested that Paul should have used "flesh" *(sarx)* in 1 Corinthians 15:44 to express physical resurrection. But Gundry notes that "Paul avoids 'flesh' in writing about the resurrection of human beings simply because the term may connote weakness, not because he wants to avoid the physical resurrection."[1] However, Paul's companion, Luke, does use the word *sarx* of the resurrection body in Luke 24:39 and Acts 2:31. But even Paul used it interchangeably with body in one resurrection passage (1 Cor. 15:38–40). In these passages the context protects it from being understood in any weak sense by stressing God's power in the resurrection and Christ's exaltation resulting from it (see especially Acts 2:31–33).

Its Immortal Nature

In addition to the physical nature of the resurrection body, evangelicals have also affirmed its immortal and imperishable dimension (1 Cor. 15:42f.), because it is a body dominated by the spirit *(soma pnuematikon,* see 1 Cor. 15:44).[2] It is not merely a resuscitated body, which is mortal and dies again. While remaining a physical body, the resurrection body is a glorified and heavenly body (Phil. 3:21; 1 John 3:2). It is specially suited for heaven, where perishable "flesh and blood" cannot enter (1 Cor. 15:50). Indeed, Jesus was the "firstfruits" of the resurrection (v. 20), the very first one to have a permanent, imperishable resurrection body.

His physical corpse was brought back to life, not by mere resuscitation, but in glorious resurrection. He was not raised in a mortal body, but in an immortal one. Thus, at the moment of resurrection the believer's body, like Christ's, will be "transformed" from a perishable to an imperishable body (v. 51).

The resurrection body is a supernatural body (v. 44). It can appear and disappear immediately (Luke 24:31, 36). It can enter rooms with closed doors (John 20:26). However, while His resurrection body can do more than a mere natural body, it is not *less* than a natural body. What is unique about the resurrection body is its possession of *immortality* (1 Cor. 15:42). Christ was not the first to be raised in a material body (John 11:43–44), but He was the first to be raised in an *imperishable* material body (1 Cor. 15:54; 2 Tim. 1:10). All others who were raised from the dead in the Bible died again. Christ was raised never to die again (1 Cor. 15:20).

Evidence for the Physical Resurrection Body

There is overwhelming support in Scripture for the belief that Christ's resurrection body is a literal, material body of flesh and bones.

The Empty Tomb

Combined with the appearances of the same crucified Christ, the empty tomb is a strong indication of the physical nature of the resurrection body of Christ. The angels said, "He is not here; for He is risen, as He said. Come, see the place where the Lord lay" (Matt. 28:6 NKJV). Later, Peter entered the tomb and "saw the strips of linen lying there, as well as the burial cloth that had been around Jesus' head. The cloth was folded up by itself, separate from the linen" (John 20:6–7 NIV). Such details reveal that the literal, physical body of Jesus that once had lain in the tomb had been resurrected (Acts 13:29–30).

A. T. Robertson concludes, from the fact that the disciples saw the head cloth that had been around His head in a place by itself, that "It was arranged in an orderly fashion [*entetuligmenon*]. There was no haste."[3] This deliberate folding of His head cloth indicates a physical act of a physical body rather than the invisible passage of an immaterial body through untouched clothes. So convincing was this evidence of a physical resurrection, that when John saw it, he believed Jesus had risen before he ever saw Him (John 20:8).

Jesus Was Touched and Handled

Jesus challenged Thomas, "Put your finger here; see my hands. *Reach out your hand and put it into my side*" (John 20:27 NIV, emphasis mine). Thomas responded (v. 28), "My Lord and My God!" Mary was clinging to Jesus after His resurrection, when He said to her, "Do not *hold on to me*, for I have not yet returned to the Father" (John 20:17 NIV, emphasis mine). Matthew says the women "*clasped his [Jesus'] feet* and worshiped him" (Matt. 28:9 NIV, emphasis mine). On another occasion Jesus said, "look at my hands and my feet. It is I myself! *Touch me* and see" (Luke 24:39 NIV, emphasis mine). John the apostle said of Christ,

> That which was from the beginning, which we have heard, which we have seen with our eyes, which we have looked at and *our hands have touched*—this we proclaim concerning the Word of life (1 John 1:1 NIV, emphasis mine).

These passages leave no room for views which *deny* that Jesus' body both before and after the resurrection was by nature a literal, material body that could be handled and touched.

Jesus' Flesh and Bones

Jesus' resurrection body was a physical body of "flesh and bones." He said emphatically, "Touch me and see; a ghost does not have *flesh and bones,* as you see I have" (Luke 24:39 NIV, emphasis mine). Then to prove to the disciples that He had a real physical body, "They gave him a piece of broiled fish, and *he took it and ate it in their presence*" (vv. 41–42 NIV, emphasis mine).

It is true that Paul said that *corruptible* "flesh and blood cannot inherit the kingdom of God" (1 Cor. 15:50 NIV). But Jesus did not have *corruptible* flesh; He was sinless (2 Cor.

5:21; Heb. 4:15). Jesus was not fleshly in the sense of sinful, but He was fleshy. He did not have *sinful* human flesh (Heb. 4:15), but He both died and rose in actual human flesh (*sarx*, see Acts 2:31).⁴ Stressing Jesus' continuing incarnation in the flesh (before and after His resurrection), John warned that "Many deceivers, who do not acknowledge Jesus Christ as coming [and remaining]⁵ in the flesh, have gone out into the world" (2 John 7 NIV).

Jesus Ate Four Times

Another convincing proof of the physical, material nature of the resurrection of Christ is that He ate food on at least four occasions as a demonstration of his resurrection. Jesus ate dinner with the two disciples (Luke 24:30). He ate later that evening with the ten apostles (Luke 24:42–43). Jesus ate breakfast with the seven apostles (John 21:12–13). Finally, He ate with all the apostles just before His ascension (Acts 1:4).

Not only did Jesus eat physical food—angels sometimes did that (Gen. 18), but He offered it as proof of the material nature of his resurrection body.⁶ No angel ever did that. Angels are spirits by nature (Heb. 1:14). Their appearances in visible form are miraculous and not representative of their natural state. Jesus' resurrection body, however, was material by nature. He said emphatically, "Touch me and see; a ghost does not have flesh and bones, as you see I have" (Luke 24:39 NIV). When the disciples supposed that they had seen a spirit, rather than Christ in His resurrection body, Jesus "showed them his hands and feet" and said, "Do you have anything here to eat?" They gave Him some fish, "and he took it and ate it in their presence" (Luke 24:38–43 NIV).

Given this context, it would have been sheer deception on Jesus' part to have offered His ability to eat physical food as a proof of His bodily resurrection if He had not been resurrected in a physical body.⁷

The fact that Jesus had a physical body that could eat was such a significant proof of His literal resurrection body that Peter included it in his short summary of the ministry of

Christ in Acts 10, where he declared that the apostles *"ate and drank with him after he rose from the dead"* (Acts 10:41 NIV).

Jesus' Resurrection Body Has Wounds

Another unmistakable evidence of the material nature of the resurrection body is the fact that it still has the physical wounds from Jesus' crucifixion. Jesus said to Thomas, "Put your fingers here; see my hands. Reach out your hand and put it into my side. Stop doubting and believe" (John 20:27 NIV). Indeed, in this same body Jesus ascended into heaven, where He is still seen as "a Lamb, looking as if it had been slain" (Rev. 5:6 NIV). When Christ returns again, it will be "this same Jesus, who has been taken from you into heaven" (Acts 1:11 NIV). Even the physical scars of His crucifixion will be visible at His Second Coming, as John declared: "Look, he is coming with the clouds, and every eye will see him, even those who pierced him" (Rev. 1:7 NIV). The body that was resurrected is the same material body that died. And it is the same physical body that resurrected and ascended into heaven that will return literally to earth at the Second Advent of our Lord (Acts 1:10–11).

Jesus' Resurrection Body Is Recognizable

Jesus was physically recognizable in His resurrection body. The usual words for "seeing" *(horao, theoreo)* and "recognizing" *(epiginosko)* physical objects are used over and over again concerning his resurrection body (see Matt. 28:7, 17; Mark 16:7; Luke 24:24; John 20:14; 1 Cor. 9:1). Indeed, His resurrection body had the same scars of His crucifixion (John 20:27). This marks it as unmistakably the same body in which He died.

It is true that occasionally Jesus was not initially recognized by some of the disciples. There are different reasons for this, some natural and perhaps some supernatural. Luke said of one occasion that "their eyes were restrainted, so that they did not know Him" (Luke 24:16 NKJV) and later "their eyes were opened and they knew Him" (v. 31 NKJV). However, sometimes there were natural factors as well. Once their perplexity (Luke 24:17-21) or sorrow (John 20:11-15) may have hindered them. Difficulty in recognizing Jesus also resulted from the dimness of the light (John 20:14-15) or the visual distance (John 21:4). On one occasion they were startled by the suddenness of Jesus' appearance (Luke 24:36-37). He also had different clothes on after the resurrection, since His other garments had been taken at the crucifixion (John 19:23-24). Finally, the initial inability to recognize Jesus may have been due in part to the fact that the disciples were spiritually dull (Luke 24:25-26) and disbelieving (John 20:24-25). However, the fact that they eventually recognized Him from His appearance, voice, scars, and the like is ample indication that He was resurrected in the same physical body in which He had died.

Jesus' Resurrection Body Could Be Seen and Heard

Not only was Jesus' resurrection body one that could be touched and handled, it was one that could be seen and heard. Matthew recorded that "when they *saw* Him, they worshiped Him" (Matt. 28:17 NKJV). The two disciples "recognized"[8] Him while eating together (see Luke 24:31), perhaps from His *physical actions* (see v. 35). The Greek word for "recognize" *(epiginosko)* means to know, to understand, or to recognize. This is a normal term for recognizing a physical object (see Mark 6:33, 54; Acts 3:10). Mary may have recognized Jesus from the tone of *His voice* (John 20:15-16). Thomas eventually recognized Jesus from His *crucifixion scars* (John 20:27-28). All the disciples saw and heard Him over a forty-day period, during which He gave "many convincing proofs" that He was alive (Acts 1:3; see also 4:2, 20).

Continuity between Jesus' Dead and Resurrected Body

Another evidence of the material nature of Jesus' resurrection body is the close and repeated connection made in the New Testament between the death and resurrection of Christ. Paul considered it of "first importance" that "Christ died for our sins, . . . that he was buried, that he was raised on the third day . . ." (1 Cor. 15:3, 4 NIV). This same connection between the physical body that was buried and the body that was resurrected is repeated elsewhere. For example, in Romans Paul declares that what was "buried" was "raised from death" (Rom. 6:3–5; Col. 2:12; see also Acts 2:23–24; 3:15; 4:10; 5:30; 10:39–40; 13:29–30). It is noteworthy that, "as an ex-Pharisee, Paul could not have used such traditional language without recognizing its intent to portray the raising of a corpse."[9]

Jesus stressed the continuity between the pre- and post-resurrection body when He said, "Destroy this temple [His body], and I will raise *it* again in three days" (John 2:19 NIV). Here Jesus declared that the same body that would be destroyed would be raised again. The same continuity is affirmed in the strong comparison between Jesus' death and resurrection and Jonah (Matt. 12:39; 16:4). He said, "For *as* Jonah was three days and three nights in the belly of the great fish, *so will* the Son of Man be three days and three nights in the heart of the earth" (Matt. 12:40 NKJV). Obviously, in both cases the same physical body that went in was the one that came out. The inseparable connection by Paul, the converted Pharisee, of the pre- and post-resurrection body of Jesus is strong confirmation that he is affirming the physical, material nature of the resurrection body. Even Professor Murray Harris, who denies the material nature of the resurrection body, admits that "in Jewish thought the idea of a Resurrection shortly after death necessarily involved (at least) the revival of the physical body, the emptying of the grave"[10] (see Appendix E).

Resurrection from among the Dead Bodies

Another biblical phrase strongly supports the view that the resurrection body was material in nature. Resurrection is often described as "from (Greek, *ek*) the dead" (Mark 9:9; Luke 24:46; John 2:22; Acts 3:15; Rom. 4:24; 1 Cor. 15:12). This means that Jesus was resurrected out from among the dead bodies, that is, from the grave where corpses are buried (Acts 13:29–30). This same phrase is used to describe Lazarus's being raised "from the dead" (John 12:1). And there is no doubt that Lazarus came out of the grave in the same material body in which he was buried. This makes it clear that the phrase refers to resurrection of a physical corpse out of a tomb or graveyard. Again, "for one who had been a Pharisee, such phraseology could carry only one meaning—physical resurrection."[11]

Continuity between the Body Sown and Raised

First Corinthians 15:35–44 implies an intrinsic identity between the physical body that is buried and the physical body that is resurrected. Paul compares the pre- and post-resurrection states to a seed that is sown and the plant that comes from it, and which is in material continuity with it. This analogy strongly suggests a material identity between the pre- and post-resurrection body. The text says clearly, "*the body* that is sown is perishable, *it* is raised imperishable; . . ." (v. 42 NIV, emphasis mine). The body that is resurrected is the *same* body that was sown (buried). If a material body was buried and an immaterial body (with different physical essence and characteristics) was raised, then it would not be one and the same body. But in this text Paul clearly affirms the identity between the pre- and post-resurrection body.

Loved Ones Will Be Physically Recognized in Heaven

The believer's resurrection body will be like Christ's (see Phil. 3:21). Since the Bible indicates that we will recognize our loved ones in heaven, we can assume that we all will have physical bodies in the resurrection. Therefore, Christ's resurrection body, after which ours are to be fashioned, must also be a physical, material body.

Paul encouraged the Thessalonian Christians whose loved ones had died that they would be reunited with them in the resurrection (1 Thess. 4:13–18; compare 1 Cor. 15:18). This comfort would make little sense if they could not recognize their loved ones in their resurrection bodies. Jesus also implied that a husband and wife would recognize each other in their resurrection bodies (see Matt. 22:23–30). In view of these passages, there is no justification for the claim that the pre- and post-resurrection body has no "material identity" and "the resurrection body will not have the anatomy or physiology of the earthly body . . . ."[12]

The New Testament Use of *Soma* (Body)

When referring to an individual human, the New Testament Greek word *for (soma)* is always used of a physical body. Paul also uses *soma* to describe the resurrection body of Christ (1 Cor. 15:42–44), thus indicating his belief that it was a physical body. The definitive exegetical work on *soma* was done by Professor Robert Gundry.[13] As evidence of the physical nature of the resurrection body, he points to "Paul's exceptionless use of *soma* for a physical body."[14] He concludes that "the consistent and exclusive use of *soma* for the physical body in anthropological contexts resists dematerialization of the resurrection, whether by idealism or by existentialism."[15]

For those who think Paul should have used another word[16] to express physical resurrection, Gundry responds, "Paul uses *soma* precisely because the physicality of the resurrection is central to his soteriology."[17] This consistent use of the word *soma* for a physical body is further confirmation that the resurrection body of Christ was by nature a literal, physical body.

The Same Body

The biblical evidence that Jesus was raised in the same physical, material body placed in the tomb is unequivocal. Not only was the tomb where the body had lain permanently empty, but the same person (Jesus) who had died appeared repeatedly after that in the same body, crucifixion scars and all. He was seen, heard, and touched with the physical senses. He declared his body was one of "flesh and bones" and offered as proof his ability to eat physical food and to be touched by physical hands. Jesus literally exhausted the ways in which he could prove that He had a real material body.

In view of this overwhelming evidence that Jesus was raised

in the very same material body in which He died, any denial of this essential of orthodox Christianity is clearly unbiblical. Evangelicals who compromise on such a fundamental doctrine deny biblical truth and are unorthodox at this point.

As we shall see in the next chapter, orthodox confessions on the "bodily resurrection" down through the centuries affirm Christ's physical, bodily resurrection. However "current" or "appealing," we should not allow fascinating deviations from this orthodoxy to gain a foothold in the evangelical church. The physical resurrection is an essential of Christian belief (see Chapter 2).

In order to defend the "faith which was once for all delivered to the saints" (Jude 3 NKJV), we must take our stand firmly on the foundation of the apostolic confession of belief in "the resurrection of the flesh."

4

"I Believe in the . . . Resurrection of the Flesh"

The Apostles' Creed declares "I believe in the . . . resurrection of the flesh." The Christian Church has always confessed its belief in the physical resurrection of Christ. Historically, this was expressed in the unmistakably clear phrase, "the resurrection of the *flesh*." In his classic work *The Nature of the Resurrection Body* (1964), J. A. Schep wrote: "We may say, therefore, that the entire early Church, in the West and in the East alike, publicly confessed belief in the resurrection of the flesh." And "in the Western creeds . . . this confessional formula has retained its place with hardly any exception. Up to the Reformation there is no exception at all."[1] Further, "the Churches of the East retained the expression 'the resurrection of the flesh' up to the Council of Constantinople in 381." When it was dropped, it was, according to Schep, "without any intention to reject the Western formulations as unscriptural, [the Eastern Church simply] went her own way in formulating the truth."[2]

Confessions of the Bodily Resurrection in the Early Church

As we saw in Chapter 3, the New Testament explicitly refers to the resurrection body as a body of flesh (Luke 24:39; Acts 2:31; compare 13:37). Several other passages directly

51

imply that Jesus' incarnation into flesh continues even after the resurrection (John 1:14; 1 John 4:2). It was after Jesus' resurrection that John warned of "many deceivers, who do not acknowledge Jesus Christ as coming [and remaining] in the flesh" (2 John 7 NIV, Greek present tense). Deceivers have persisted throughout church history. At each age, Christians have declared the truth in opposition to error.

Irenaeus (c. A.D. 130–200)

With the exception of unorthodox views, such as that of Origen (see Chapter 6), the earliest church fathers consistently affirmed that Jesus rose in the same body of flesh in which He was crucified. Irenaeus was one of the first great theologians of the Christian Church. In his famous work *Against Heresies,* he said,

> The Church [believes] in one God, the Father Almighty, Maker of heaven and earth, and the sea, and all things that are in them: and in one Christ Jesus, the Son of God, who became incarnate for our salvation; . . . and the resurrection from the dead, and ascension into heaven in the *flesh* of the beloved Christ Jesus, our Lord . . . (emphasis mine).[3]

In this confession Irenaeus made it clear that Jesus' resurrection in literal human flesh was a universal belief of the early church. He added, "Inasmuch as Christ did rise in our *flesh,* it follows that we shall be also raised in the same [flesh]; since the resurrection promised to us should not be referred to spirits naturally immortal, but to bodies in themselves mortal (emphasis mine)."[4] Resurrecting the flesh is no problem for God. For, "since the Lord has power to infuse life into what He has fashioned, since the *flesh* is capable of being quickened, what remains to prevent its participation in incorruption, which is a blissful and never–ending life granted by God (emphasis mine)?"[5]

Tertullian (c. A.D. 160–230)

Writing in his *Prescription Against Heretics,* the converted lawyer from north Africa, Quintus Septimus Tertullian declared the resurrection of the flesh to be normative for the Church:

> Now with regard to this rule of faith . . . you must know, that which prescribes the belief that there is one only God, and that He is none other than the Creator of the world, who produced all things out of nothing through His own Word, first of all sent forth; . . . at last brought down by the Spirit and Power of the Father into the Virgin Mary, was made flesh in her womb, . . . having been crucified, He rose again the third day; . . . will come with glory to take the saints to the enjoyment of everlasting life and of the heavenly promises, and to condemn the wicked to everlasting fire, after the resurrection of both these classes shall have happened, together with the restoration of their *flesh* (emphasis mine).[6]

Tertullian added that "this rule, as it will be proved, was taught by Christ, and raises amongst ourselves no other question than those which heresies introduce, and which make men heretics."[7] This makes it clear that the belief in the material nature of the resurrection body was considered to be the teaching of Christ, the universal rule of the Christian Church, and those who denied it were considered heretics.

Justin Martyr (c. A.D. 100–165)

The converted philosopher Justin Martyr was one of the great apologists of the early Church. He not only used the phrase "resurrection of the flesh," but he also designated it as referring to the flesh-body, not to the soul. He said plainly, "the resurrection is a resurrection of the *flesh* which dies (emphasis mine)."[8] He added, "There are some who maintain that even Jesus Himself appeared only as spiritual, and not in *flesh* (emphasis mine), but presented merely the appearance of flesh: these persons seek to rob the flesh of the promise."[9] To them Justin replied: "Let the unbelieving be silent, even though they themselves do not believe. But in truth, He has even called the *flesh* to the resurrection, and promises to it everlasting life. For where He promises to save man, there He gives the promise to the *flesh* (emphasis mine)."[10]

As to Jesus' resurrection, Justin asked, "Why did he rise in the *flesh* in which He suffered, unless to show the resurrection of the *flesh?* (emphasis mine)"[11] Furthermore,

> when He had thus shown them that there is truly a resurrection of the *flesh*, wishing to show them this also, that it is not impossible for *flesh* to ascend into heaven . . . . "He was taken up into heaven while they beheld," as He was in the *flesh* (emphasis mine).[12]

Justin left no doubt that he believed that the literal, physical flesh of Christ both raised and ascended into heaven.

Athenagoras (Second Century)

Writing in a treatise on "The Resurrection of the Dead," the second century Christian teacher at Athens, Athenagoras, distinguished between the spiritual dimension of man and the flesh-body dimension, which he believed died and rose from the dead. In response to those who denied the physical resurrection he declared,

> Moreover also, that His power is sufficient of the raising of dead bodies, is shown by the creation of these *same bodies*. For if, when they did not exist, He made at their first formation the bodies of men, and *their original elements*, He will, when they are dissolved, in whatever manner that may take place, raise them again with equal ease: for this too, is equally possible to Him (emphasis mine).[13]

So literally did he take the nature of the resurrection body that he believed even the "original elements" of the body would be restored at the resurrection. And although this specificity is unnecessary to an orthodox view (see Appendix A), nonetheless, it does show the unmistakable belief that the resurrection body was the same material body that had died.

Rufinus (A.D. 345–410)

This famous Latin bishop wrote a "Commentary on the Apostles' Creed." In it he declared that even the lost particles of the dead body would be restored in the resurrection body. In another statement by Rufinus found in a preface to "Pamphilus' Defense of Origen," he emphasized the identity of Christ's body and His flesh, saying,

> We believe that it is *this very flesh* in which we are now living which will rise again, not one kind of flesh instead of another, nor another body than the body of *this flesh* . . . . It is an absurd invention of maliciousness to think that the human body is different from the *flesh* . . . (emphasis mine).[14]

It is obvious that Rufinus made no subtle distinction between body and flesh, such as some modern scholars make in denying the material nature of the resurrection body. A body is a body of flesh, and flesh is that of which a body is composed. Nothing could be more plain.

Epiphanius (Fourth Century)

The *Second Creed of Epiphanius* (A.D. 374) is an enlargement of the famous *Nicene Creed* by the learned Bishop of Salamis, Cyprus, named Epiphanius. It affirmed that Christ went into heaven in the same body of flesh in which He suffered:

> For the Word became *flesh*, not undergoing any change nor converting Godhead into Manhood, [but] uniting into his own one holy perfection and Godhead, . . . the same suffered in the flesh; rose again; and went up to heaven in the *same body*, sat down gloriously at the right hand of the Father; is coming in the *same body* in glory to judge the quick and the dead; . . . (emphasis mine).[15]

Three things are evident from this. First, this creed confessed that Christ was resurrected in the same "flesh" in which He was crucified. Second, "flesh" is used interchangeably with "body." After all, a human body is a body of flesh. And Epiphanius believed that to deny that Jesus had a fleshy human body either before or after the resurrection was to deny the incarnation itself (see John 1:14; 1 John 4:2). Third, this same body of flesh in which Jesus lived and died is now in heaven and will return again to earth at the Second Coming.

Cyril of Jerusalem (A.D. 315–386)

In his famous *Catechetical Lectures* (Chapter 18), the bishop of Jerusalem argued that God is able to reconstitute flesh which has become dust into *flesh* again. He considered it heretical to deny that one is resurrected in the same material body in which he died.

> Let no heretic ever persuade thee to speak evil of the Resurrection. For to this day the Manichees say, that the resurrection of the Saviour was phantom-wise, and not real, not heeding Paul who says, *Who was made flesh of the seed of David according to flesh;* and again, *By the resurrection of Jesus Christ our Lord from the dead* (emphasis mine).[16]

According to Cyril, belief in the material nature of the resurrection body was part of the confession of the "one Holy Catholic Church."

> The Faith which we rehearse contains in order the following, "AND IN ONE BAPTISM OF REPENTANCE FOR THE REMISSION OF SINS; AND IN ONE HOLY CATHOLIC CHURCH; AND IN THE *RESURRECTION OF THE FLESH;* AND IN ETERNAL LIFE (emphasis mine)."[17]

Cyril referred to the resurrection body as "the very same body" we have before the resurrection.[18] Similar views were held by Gregory of Nazianzen (a president of the Constantinople Council), Gregory of Nyssa, and Basil the Great. From this it is evident that even the early Eastern Church confessed a literal, material resurrection body.

Confessions of the Bodily Resurrection in the Medieval Church

The earliest great father of the Middle Ages was the Bishop of Hippo, St. Augustine. His extensive and influential writings dominated the medieval church and continue to influence Christian thought even to this day.

Saint Augustine (A.D. 354–430)

Augustine spoke most explicitly to the nature of the resurrection body in this passage: "It is indubitable that the resurrection of Christ, and His ascension into heaven with the *flesh* in which He rose, is already preached and believed in the whole world (emphasis mine)."[19] In the same place Augustine added that the belief in the resurrection of the material body of flesh was a universal belief in the Church:

> The world has come to the belief that the *earthly body* of Christ was received up into heaven. Already both the learned and unlearned have believed in the resurrection of the *flesh* and its ascension to the heavenly places, while only a very few either of the educated or uneducated are still staggered by it.[20]

Augustine also stressed the fact that resurrection is in the same physical body in which one lived before death and then the resurrection. He declared that individuals would be raised in their same sex and even without any bodily loss, "lest the men who largest here should lose anything of their bulk and it should perish, in contradiction to the words of Christ, who said that not a hair of their head should perish . . . ."[21]

Along with the early Fathers, Augustine believed that God would reconstitute all of the decomposed parts of the body in the resurrection, saying,

> Far be it from us to fear that the omnipotence of the Creator cannot, for *the resuscitation and reanimation of our bodies, recall all the portions which have been consumed* by beasts or fire, or have been dissolved into dust or ashes, or have decomposed into water, or even evaporated into the air (emphasis mine).[22]

St. Augustine left no doubt about the universal Christian belief in the literal, physical nature of the resurrection body. It was the same material body, now glorified, that was possessed before the resurrection.[23]

St. Anselm (A.D. 1033–1109)

Without interruption from Augustine to Anselm, the catholic (universal) confession of the Christian Church was of the resurrection of the actual physical body of flesh and bones. Speaking to the topic "How man will rise with the *same body* which he has in this world," the great theologian St. Anselm of Canterbury concluded,

> From this the future resurrection of the dead is clearly proved. For if man is to be perfectly restored, the restoration should make him such as he would have been had he never sinned . . . . Therefore, as man, had he not sinned, was to have been transferred with the *same body* to an immortal state, so when he shall be restored, it must properly be *with his own body as he lived in this world* (emphasis mine).[24]

Adding an insightful comment on what constitutes human nature, Anselm declared,

> I do not think mortality inheres in the essential nature of man, but only as corrupted. Since, had man never sinned, and had immortality been unchangeably confirmed, he would have been as really man: and, when the dying rise again, incorruptible, *they will be no less really men.* For, if mortality was an essential attribute of human nature, then he who was immortal could not be man (emphasis mine).[25]

From Anselm's statements it is evident that he believed that in the resurrection believers will be "no less really men" but will have the same "essential nature," including both the "body and soul"[26] they had before the resurrection.

St. Thomas Aquinas (A.D. 1224–1274)

Capping off the end of the medieval church was the great systematic theologian Thomas Aquinas. On the nature of the resurrection body, he said explicitly: "The soul does not take an airy or heavenly body, or a body of another organic constitution, but a human body composed of *flesh and bones* and the same members enjoyed at present (emphasis mine)."[27]

Commenting on those who deny a physical resurrection, Aquinas wrote,

> They have not believed in the resurrection of the body, and have strained to twist the words of Holy Scripture to mean a spiritual resurrection, a resurrection from sin through grace . . that St. Paul believed in a *bodily resurrection* is clear . . . to deny this, and *to affirm a purely spiritual resurrection is against the Christian Faith* (emphasis mine).[28]

As for the seeming impossibility that a body that dies could be restored with numerical identity, Aquinas concluded that "by conjunction to a soul numerically the same *the man will be restored to matter numerically the same* (emphasis mine)."[29] Therefore, "although this corporeality yields to nothingness when the human body is corrupted, it cannot, for all that, be an obstacle to *the body's rising with numerical identity* (81.7 emphasis mine).[30] Hence, "it is clear that *man returns numerically the same both by reason of the permanence of the rational soul and by reason of the unity of matter*" (81.10 emphasis mine).[31]

The fact that human bodies have parts that are changing "is not an obstacle to his being numerically one from the beginning of his life to the end of it, . . . for the form and species of its single parts remain continuously through a whole life" (81.12).[32] From this "it is clear, also, that there is no obstacle to faith in the resurrection—even in the fact that some men eat human flesh. . . ." For in the resurrection "*the flesh consumed will rise in him in whom it was first perfected by a rational soul* (emphasis mine)." As for those who ate flesh, that will not be part of their resurrection body, "what is wanting will be supplied by the Creator's omnipotence" (81.13).[33] These unequivocally clear statements leave no doubt that Aquinas believed that the resurrection body was numerically identical to the pre-resurrection body.

Confessions of the Bodily Resurrection from the Reformation to the Present

The Reformers did not forsake their orthodox Christological roots. They too continued the unbroken confession of the resurrection of the flesh. Consider the following examples.

The Formula of Concord (A.D. 1576)

This great Lutheran confession reads as follows:

> We believe, teach and confess . . . the chief articles of our faith (of Creation, of Redemption, of Sanctification, and the Resurrection of the *flesh*) . . . (emphasis mine).[34]
>
> This same human nature of ours (that is his own work) Christ has redeemed, the same (inasmuch as it is his own work) he sanctifies, the *same [human nature] doth he raise from the dead*, and with great glory (as being his own) doth he crown it (emphasis mine).[35]

The Saxon Visitation Articles (A.D. 1592)

These Articles, prepared by Aegidius Hunnius and other Lutheran theologians in Saxony, declare,

> By this personal union [of Christ's two natures], and the exaltation which followed it, Christ, according to the *flesh*, is placed at the right hand of God, and has received power in heaven and earth, and is made partaker of all the divine majesty, honor, power, and glory (emphasis mine).[36]

The French Confession of Faith (A.D. 1559)

This confession was prepared by John Calvin and his student, De Chandieu. It was approved by the Synod of Paris in 1559. On the resurrection it pronounced that "although Jesus Christ, in rising from the dead, bestowed immortality upon *his body*, yet he did not take away from it the truth of *its nature*, and we so consider him in his divinity that we do not despoil him of his humanity (emphasis mine)."[37] This confession is of particular interest since it speaks explicitly to the point that the resurrection did not take away from the nature of the physical body, but simply added immortality to it. To deny this would be a denial of Jesus' humanity.

The Belgic Confession (A.D. 1561)

This confession was composed in French for the churches in Flanders and the Netherlands. It was adopted by the Reformed Synod at Emden (1571) and the Synod of Dort (1619). On the resurrection it says,

> And though he hath by his resurrection given immortality to the same, nevertheless he hath not changed the reality of his human nature; forasmuch as our salvation and resurrection also depend on the *reality of his body* (emphasis mine).[38]
>
> Finally, we believe, according to the Word of God, . . . that our Lord Jesus Christ will come from heaven, *corporally* and visibly as he ascended with great glory and majesty, to declare himself Judge of the quick and the dead, ... For all the dead shall be raised out of the earth, and their souls joined and united with *their proper bodies in which they formerly lived* (emphasis mine).[39]

From these statements it is evident that they believed our salvation and resurrection depend on Christ's resurrection in the same physical, material body possessed before the resurrection.

The Thirty-Nine Articles of Religion (A.D. 1562)

These Articles of the Church of England were adopted in 1562 and revised for the Protestant Episcopal Church in the United States in 1801. Both versions declare that:

> Christ did truly *rise* again from death, and *took again his body, with flesh and bones,* and all things appertaining to the perfection of Man's nature; wherewith he ascended into Heaven, and there sitteth, until he return to judge all Men at the last day (emphasis mine).[40]

This could scarcely be more explicit about the material nature of the resurrection body. Christ arose in the exact same body of "flesh and bones" in which He had lived and died. And it is this same body "wherewith" He ascended into heaven.

The Westminster Confession (A.D. 1647)

The Westminster Confession first appeared in England in 1647. It has been the standard for orthodox Presbyterians since that time. The article on the resurrection of Christ (VII, 4) also affirms the historic belief in the physical nature of His resurrection body, confessing that He "was crucified, and died; was buried, and remained under the power of death, *yet saw no corruption. On the third day he arose from the dead, with the same body in which he suffered; with which he ascended into heaven,* and there sitteth at the right hand of his Father . . . (emphasis mine)."[41]

Here again the language is clear: The resurrection body was the same physical body Jesus had before His death. In fact, that body saw no corruption, so it had to be the same material body.

Declaration of the Congregational Union (1833)

Early Congregationalists and Baptists also held to the physical, material nature of the resurrection. The Declaration of the Congregational Union of England and Wales (1833) speaks of Christ being "manifested in the *flesh*" and "after his death and resurrection, he ascended up into heaven . . . ." Referring to the material bodies of the departed, they add: "And the bodies of the dead will be raised again."[42] The New Hampshire Baptist Confession (1833) also acknowledged the material nature of the resurrection body, speaking of raising "the dead from the grave" where the material corpse was buried.[43] Other Anabaptist and Baptist groups also confessed the literal physical nature of the resurrection body.[44]

It was not until 1552 that the phrase "resurrection of the body" was admitted to the Apostles' Creed as an alternate reading for "the resurrection of the flesh." But as Schep notes, even here "the terms 'flesh' and 'body' were regarded as equivalent." In his helpful work *The Resurrection of the Flesh*, L. E. Block also defends the phrase "resurrection of the flesh" as "legitimate expression of the Biblical doctrine of the resurrection."[45] Indeed, as we have seen, affirming the resurrection of the flesh is not only the biblical teaching on the resurrection but has been the universal confession of the orthodox Church down through the centuries.

The Heart of the Issue

From this discussion of the great confessions on the "resurrection of the flesh," several key elements of the orthodox view emerge. There are at least three of them explicitly stated (and others implied):

1) Jesus resurrected in the *same body* in which He died.
2) The resurrection body was *material* by nature.
3) The resurrection was an *historical (space–time) event*.

Numerical Identity (The Same Physical Body)

It has always been part of orthodox belief to acknowledge that Jesus was raised immortal in the *same physical body* in which He died. That is, His *resurrection body was numerically the same as His pre-resurrection body*. Sometimes they used the very words "numerically identical." At other times they indicated it by calling it "the same body" or equivalent expressions.

Materiality

The *resurrection body is a material body*. It is not invisible or immaterial by nature. The orthodox fathers unanimously confessed belief in "the *resurrection of the flesh*." They believed that flesh was essential to human nature and that Jesus, being fully human, was not only incarnated in, but also resurrected in, the same human flesh He had before His death. A resurrected body can be seen with the naked eye. If a picture were taken of it, the image would appear on the film. As Anselm affirmed, it is just as material as Adam's body was and would have remained if Adam had not sinned. It was so physical that were someone to have seen it arise in the tomb, it would have caused dust to fall off the slab from which it arose!

Historicity

Jesus' resurrection was a *historical event*. It happened in the space-time world. From the very earliest Christian documents it is dated as "on the third day" (see 1 Cor. 15:4). The body that was raised was empirically observable. Thus, the stress is laid upon his physical appearances (see 1 Cor. 15:5–7). Paul said, "Have I not seen Jesus our Lord?" (1 Cor. 9:1 NIV). John stressed that he "became flesh," He "was in the world" (John 1:10, 14), and He remained "in the flesh" even after His resurrection (1 John 4:2; 2 John 7). Regardless of the supernatural nature of the event, the resurrection was as much a part of history as was His incarnation before His death.

Strangely, even some who deny this orthodox confession of the resurrection of the numerically identical material body of Jesus in the space-time world, admit: "Until the time of the Reformation the creeds of the West spoke only of the resurrection of the flesh *(sarkos anastasis; resurrectio carnis)*. Here 'flesh' refers to the material components, the substance, or the body: the flesh-body as distinct from the soul (emphasis mine).[46]

In spite of this admission, they affirm just the opposite of the orthodox view, claiming that:

1) It is not numerically identical to pre-resurrection body.

The new body is qualitatively and numerically distinct from the old body (emphasis mine).[47]

2) Jesus was not resurrected in the flesh.

It will be neither fleshly nor fleshy (emphasis added).[48]

3) Jesus' resurrection body was not a visible object in the observable world.[49]

After his resurrection his essential state was one of invisibility and immateriality (emphasis mine).[50]

As a non-empirical event of and with Jesus himself after his death, the resurrection is *per se* trans-historical . . . (emphasis mine).[51]

The Resurrection of the Flesh

All the essential characteristics of the resurrection body are summed up well in the phrase "resurrection of the flesh." However, as we have already seen (Chapter 3), the New Testament speaks directly of the resurrection body as "flesh" in some passages (see Luke 24:39; Acts 2:31) and inclusively in others (see 1 John 4:2; 2 John 7). Denial of the apostolic belief in the "resurrection of the flesh" is both unbiblical and contrary to the orthodox confessions of the Christian Church.

5

Denials of the Physical Resurrection

$$\text{D}$$enials of the orthodox, biblical teaching that Jesus resurrected in the same physical body in which He died are not new. Even during New Testament times, the false story circulated that Jesus' "disciples came during the night and stole his body" (Matt. 28:13 NIV). Since then, the physical resurrection has been denied in many other ways by both liberals and cultists.

Common Denials of the Resurrection

The most common denial of the resurrection of Christ is simply to argue that His body never came out of the tomb alive. This can be done in several ways. Some claim that Christ's body remained in the grave and that the disciples went to the wrong tomb. Others say the disciples stole His body. Still others modify this idea and hold that Jesus never died on the cross, He only lost consciousness. He later revived in the tomb.

The Common Element

The common element behind most of the denials of Christ's physical resurrection is the rejection of miracles as possible and real events in the space-time world. Much of modern antisupernaturalism is traceable to the Jewish pantheist Benedict Spinoza (1632–1677) and the Scottish skeptic David Hume (1711–1776).

Benedict Spinoza (1632–1677)[1]

One of the first modern thinkers to attack the supernatural was naturalist Benedict Spinoza. Misapplying Newton's concept of a universal law of nature, Spinoza insisted that "nothing then, comes to pass in nature in contravention to her universal laws, nay, nothing does not agree with them and follow from them, for . . . she keeps a fixed and immutable order." In fact for Spinoza "a miracle, whether in contravention to, or beyond, nature, is a mere absurdity." Spinoza was dogmatic about the impossibility of miracles. He proclaimed, "We may, then, be absolutely certain that every event which is truly described in Scripture necessarily happened, like everything else, according to natural laws."[2]

Spinoza's argument can be summarized as follows:

1) Miracles are violations of natural laws.
2) Natural laws are immutable (unchanging).
3) It is impossible for immutable laws to be violated.
4) Therefore, miracles are impossible.

On the basis of this argument, Spinoza rejected all miracles in the Bible, concluding that "every event . . . in Scripture necessarily happened, like everything else, according to natural laws."[3] This means there was no bodily resurrection. "The apostles who came after Christ preached it [Christianity] to all men as a universal religion *solely* in virtue of Christ's passion [death]."[4]

Few scientists today would agree with Spinoza's outdated statement on the immutability of natural laws. Modern physicists think of natural laws as being only highly probable descriptions, not absolutely unbreakable laws. Nonetheless, Spinoza's antisupernatural legacy continues.

David Hume (1711–1776)

Perhaps the most enduring argument against miracles came a century after Spinoza from the skeptic David Hume. He boasted of his argument: "I flatter myself that I have discovered an argument . . . which, if just, will, with the wise and learned, be an everlasting check to all kinds of superstitious delusion, and consequently will be useful as long as the world endures."[5]

What is the "final" argument against the miraculous? According to Hume it goes like this:

1) "A miracle is a violation of the laws of nature."
2) "Firm and unalterable experience has established these laws."
3) "A wise man proportions his belief to the evidence."
4) Therefore, "the proof against miracles . . . is as entire as any argument from experience can possibly be imagined."[6]

The key statement in this argument is the second one, which Hume explains as follows: "There must, therefore, be a uniform experience against every miraculous event. Otherwise the event would not merit that appellation." So "nothing is esteemed a miracle if it ever happened in the common course of nature."[7]

In view of his argument against miracles, Hume concluded that no miracle in the Bible is credible, including the bodily resurrection of Christ. The overwhelming testimony of our senses is that people who die do not rise again. Hence, the story of an alleged resurrection is so exceptional as to be refuted by this universal experiential testimony against it.

The Result of Denying Miracles

On the basis of this antisupernaturalism, modern biblical scholars began to write their desupernaturalized versions of the life of Christ. One of the most famous ones was that of David Strauss, *The Life of Jesus* (1835–36). He concluded emphatically: "We may summarily reject all miracles, prophecies, narratives of angels and demons, and the like, as simply impossible and irreconcilable with the known and universal laws which govern the course of events."[8]

The author of the American *Declaration of Independence* (1776), Thomas Jefferson, literally cut all the miracles out of the Gospels. The truncated version of the life of Christ was published after Jefferson's death as "The Jefferson Bible." It ends abruptly after Jesus' death with these words: "Now, in the place where he was crucified, there was a garden; and in the garden a new sepulchre, wherein was never man yet laid. There laid they Jesus, and rolled a great stone to the door of the sepulchre, and departed."[9]

Such is the result of denying miracles. It leaves us with a sealed tomb and an empty hope for a resurrected life to come.

A Response to the Case Against Miracles

The common thread in all these naturalistic attempts to explain away the bodily resurrection of Christ is their rejection of supernatural intervention into history. The arguments against miracles (and the liberal explanations in place of the resurrection based on them) is the belief that science is about regularities, not singularities. That is, a scientific understanding is only possible if something happens over and over so that a pattern develops. If something happens only once, as opposed to many times, there is no credible basis for believing in it. Science as such can never accept the miraculous, which by its very nature does not happen over and over again.

However, the regularity argument against miracles is without foundation. Even naturalistic scientists accept some major events that happened only once. They accept that the origin of the universe, the origin of first life, and the origin of new life forms are all one-time events, singularities rather than regularities.

The Universe Began Only Once

According to the prevailing Big Bang theory of the origin of the universe, all the matter of the cosmos came into existence in a gigantic cosmic explosion. The evidence for this is abundant. For example, according to the Second Law of Thermodynamics, the universe is running out of usable energy. It is literally running down. If it were eternal, its usable energy level would be static, not decreasing. However, its usable energy level *is* decreasing, therefore, it must have had a beginning.

Agnostic astronomer Robert Jastrow says the evidence that the universe began "has convinced almost the last doubting Thomas,"[10] for "the scientist's pursuit of the past ends in the *moment* of creation."[11] The universe came into existence "at a *definite moment of time,* in a flash of light and energy."[12] And it has not repeated this since. In other words, as far as the scientific evidence goes, the origin of the material universe (cosmos) is a unique, one-time event. Yet most scientists believe that it did happen. Why then should they reject a miracle because it is a one-time event that is not repeated over and over?

The Origin of Life Happened Only Once

Naturalistic scientists believe that life began on earth (or some other planet) by spontaneous generation. That is, it emerged from chemicals by purely natural processes. One scenario involves lightning combining gases into amino acids of which proteins are made which are the building blocks of life. Even though they admit that the odds against this chance development are very rare (one scientist estimated the chances as 1 in $10^{40,000}$), nevertheless, they believe it did happen.[13]

In other words, they hold that life began in the "primeval pond" just once, by chance, and, as far as we can tell, it has never emerged spontaneously again. Even though they cannot repeat it in an experiment or observe it in the world, they think it is reasonable and scientific to hold this view. But if it is credible to believe in this statistical "miracle," then they have no justification to reject a biblical miracle. Just because the resurrection of Christ is a rare and unrepeated event does not mean it is not credible.

As a matter of fact, to reject miracles one must reject God. If God exists, then miracles as defined above are possible. If there is a God who can act, then there can be acts of God. As C. S. Lewis aptly commented, "But if we admit God, must we admit Miracles? Indeed, you have no security against it. That is the bargain."[14] Furthermore, Hume was wrong when he claimed that what happened only once is infinitely improbable. For "the whole history of the Earth has also happened only once: is it therefore incredible?"[15]

Liberal Explanations Opposed to the Resurrection

Since most liberals acknowledge that Jesus lived and that there were reports from the very beginning of Christianity that Jesus rose from the dead, they must offer some explanation of the reports. From this several theories have emerged. Once one accepts the possibility of the miraculous, none of them is very credible. Nonetheless, those who deny miracles must still explain the reported resurrection of Christ.

The New Testament Documents Are Not Reliable

The reports that Jesus rose from the dead are mainly in the New Testament and many scholars deny their reliability, claiming that the accounts are legendary or mythological. Rudolph Bultmann, for example, insisted that the resurrection "is not an event of past history . . . . An historical fact which involves a resurrection from the dead is utterly inconceivable."[16] He listed four reasons for this conclusion. First of all, there is "the incredibility of a mythical event like the resurrection of a corpse—for that is what resurrection means . . . ." Second, there is "the difficulty of establishing the objective historicity of the resurrection . . . ." Third, "the resurrection is an article of faith . . . ." Finally, "such a miracle is not otherwise unknown to mythology."[17]

So, the resurrection is not an event of objective history. It is a "myth" which cannot be observed or verified. In support of his contention, Bultmann pointed to the transcendent nature of a miracle. It is an "act of God." But God is beyond space-time history. His acts are transcendent; they are above observable human history. To reduce them to empirical history is to deny their transcendent, spiritual nature, and to thereby rob them of their redemptive truth. Miracles are not of this world. They are acts in the spiritual world.

There are two basic problems with this objection, one philosophical and one historical.

Philosophical Problem

Philosophically, Bultmann wrongly assumes that because a miracle is not *of* history that it cannot be *in* history. That does not follow. Certainly there is a transcendent dimension to a miracle. The resurrection, for example, is more than a purely empirical event. It has a transcendent *source* (God) as well as a trans-historical *significance* (salvation). But because the resurrection of Christ comes from *beyond* time does not mean that it did not happen *in* time. A miracle is an act of God, and God is *beyond* the world, but He can, nevertheless, act *in* the world. They are historical and observable insofar as the resurrection and post-resurrection appearances of Christ were events in space and time. For example, the appearances of Christ were observable with the naked eye. Even the event of the resurrection could have been seen with mortal eyes. Had anyone been present in the tomb that first Easter morning, they would have seen the corpse of Jesus of Nazareth come to life and walk away.

Historical Problem

Historically, claiming that the New Testament documents are not reliable is completely unwarranted. Dr. Gary Habermas discredited this claim in his excellent book *The Verdict of History: Conclusive Evidence for the Life of Jesus*[18], as did F. F. Bruce in his popular *The New Testament Documents: Are They Reliable?*[19], and John Warwick Montgomery in his *Christianity and History*.[20]

First of all, there are more manuscripts of the New Testament than any book from the ancient world. Many classics survive on only a handful of manuscripts, but the New Testament is supported by over 5300 manuscripts. This means we have a wealth of textual information from which to reconstruct the original statements.

Second, the New Testament manuscripts are earlier than those of other books from the ancient world. The gap between the time of composition and the first copies of other books from the ancient world is about a thousand years. But the first copies of New Testament books come from only about a hundred years after the end of the first century. This means that there was insufficient time for spurious claims and myths to be added to the original without detection and challenge. It also establishes the composition of the books within the lifetimes of the witnesses.

Third, the accuracy of the copies of the New Testament is better than that of other books from the ancient world. The Hindu *Mahabharata* is only about 90 percent accurate and Homer's *Iliad* about 95 percent, but, according to the science of textual criticism, the New Testament copies are over 99 percent accurate.[21] In other words, we can be confident that what we have is what was written originally.

Fourth, the number of different writers of the New Testament is greater than those of other events from antiquity. Four persons wrote the Gospels (Matthew, Mark, Luke, and John) and at least four other persons wrote epistles (Paul, James, Peter, and Jude). The harmony and consistency of their stories confirms the stories' authenticity.

Fifth, there are six different but not conflicting accounts of the resurrected Christ (Matt. 28; Mark 16; Luke 24; John 20–21; Acts 1; 1 Cor. 15). Two or three witnesses are sufficient to establish a credible report.

Sixth, there were over five hundred people who saw Christ after His resurrection over a forty-day period of time on at least twelve different occasions. They saw Him and His empty grave, heard Him, touched Him, and even ate with Him four times (see Chapter 8). The sum total of this evidence is more than sufficient to establish the authenticity of the event.

The Disciples Stole the Body

The view that the disciples conspired to steal Jesus' body was the earliest attempt to explain away the resurrection. The soldiers at Jesus' tomb were paid a large sum of money and were told, "You are to say, 'His disciples came during the night and stole him away while we were asleep'" (Matt. 28:13 NIV). This theory was examined and refuted by the early church historian Eusebius of Caesarea in his *Demonstratio Evangelica* (314–318). In the eighteenth century the deist H. S. Reimarus (1769) revived the theory.[22] However, his thesis was completely discredited by Nathaniel Lardner's impressive twelve-volume *The Credibility of the Gospel History* (1730–55). A good recent summary of the arguments against it can be found in William Lane Craig's *Knowing the Truth About the Resurrection.*[23]

This conspiracy view lacks credibility for several reasons. For one, it is opposed to the high moral character of the disciples as honest men, taught to value honesty by their teachers, who were even willing to die for their beliefs. For another, it assumes, contrary to their unimaginative minds and good character, that the disciples were clever plotters. Furthermore, it is highly implausible to suppose that universal agreement could be maintained among all the disciples without the story eventually unraveling. The conspiracy theory is also contrary to the fact that previously they had fled for fear of being caught. Moreover, if the body actually had been stolen, the soldiers would have been disciplined for sleeping on duty, but they were not. The radical change in the disciples after the resurrection also shows they did not steal the body but were transformed by seeing Jesus alive. And finally, stealing a dead body is one thing; giving it life is another. This hypothesis does not explain the twelve appearances of this same body over the next forty days to over five hundred people (see Chapter 8).

The Women Went to the Wrong Tomb

Some have argued that in the dark of the early morning Mary Magdalene and the women went to the wrong tomb. Finding it empty, they incorrectly reported to the disciples that Christ had risen from the dead. This theory was put forth by Kirsopp Lake in *The Historical Evidence for the Resurrection of Jesus Christ* (d. 1907).[24] The converted skeptic Frank Morrison thoroughly refuted this view in his famous book *Who Moved the Stone?*[25]

This explanation holds no water for many reasons. First, if it was so dark the women could not see, then why did Mary Magdalene suppose that the one she saw was the gardener already at work? It was uncommon (and difficult) for gardeners to attempt gardening before dawn. Second, if they went to the wrong tomb in the dark, then the authorities could have gone to the right tomb in the light (where they knew Jesus was buried) and produced the body to refute the error. The fact that the authorities did not do this is strong evidence that Jesus' tomb was already empty. Third, later Peter and John went to the tomb in broad daylight and saw no body, only empty grave clothes. Fourth, like the other naturalistic explanations, this theory does not account for the twelve post-resurrection appearances of Christ (see Chapter 8), nor the miraculously transformed lives of the disciples from despondency and fear to conviction and courage within a few weeks after Christ's death.

Joseph Removed the Body

Since Jesus was buried in a borrowed tomb belonging to Joseph of Arimathea, some suppose that Joseph removed Jesus' body. However, there are serious problems with this suggestion. For example, when did he do it? In the dark with torches while guards were standing guard at the tomb's entrance? They would have seen him and stopped him. And later at dawn, the women were already there and would have seen him. Besides, why would Joseph do it? There is no plausible motive for the crime. Certainly he would not do it to keep the disciples from stealing the body. He was himself a follower of Jesus. And if he was not a disciple, then he could have produced the body and refuted the resurrection claim of Jesus' disciples. Additionally, this theory is contrary to Joseph's character as a devout follower of Christ, who taught his followers to be honest and truthful. Finally, this view does not explain the fact that this same body appeared alive on twelve occasions for the next month and a half.

The Authorities Took the Body

It has been suggested that the authorities could have stolen the body, but this is without any real justification for two very good reasons. Here again Christian writers have provided convincing arguments against this hypothesis.[26] If Roman or Jewish authorities took Jesus' body, then why did they charge that the disciples stole it? More importantly, there is nothing they would have liked better than to produce the dead body of Jesus and thereby refute this new "sect" of Christians that sprang up. If the authorities had the corpse of Jesus, they could have—and certainly would have—produced it and ended Christianity right then. But they did not have it, and Christianity spread like wild-fire in early Judaism with thousands accepting Jesus as their living Messiah (Acts 2:41; 4:4; 5:14).

Jesus Only Swooned on the Cross

One of the most popular alternatives to the resurrection is the view that Jesus didn't really die. He only swooned or fainted and later revived in the cool, damp tomb. There are other variations on this that involve Jesus taking drugs in order to feign death. All these views have the same problems.

First, they fail to take seriously the extent of Jesus' fatal wounds. He had no sleep the night before His crucifixion (Mark 14:32–41). He even collapsed carrying His cross, due to exhaustion from the sleepless night and severe beatings He received from the Roman soldiers (Mark 15:21). He had four nail wounds on His hands and feet (Luke 24:39). His side was pierced by a spear that brought forth water and blood (John 19:34). And He was on the cross from 9 A.M. until just before sunset (Mark 15:25, 33, 34). This extended time of suffering and bloodshed was fatal.

Medical evidence supports the reality of Christ's physical death. In 1847 Dr. William Stroud wrote his famous treatise *The Physiological Cause of the Death of Christ,* in which he showed that the "blood and water" that came from Jesus' spear-pierced side was indubitable proof of His physical death. Recently, *The Journal of the American Medical Society* (March 21, 1986) concluded:

> Clearly, the weight of historical and medical evidence indicates that Jesus was dead before the wound to his side was inflicted and supports the traditional view that the spear, thrust between his right ribs, probably perforated not only the

right lung but also the pericardium and heart and thereby en-
sured his death. Accordingly, interpretations based on the assumption that Jesus did not die on the cross appear to be at
odds with modern medical knowledge.[27]

Second, Jesus' death agony was heard by those around the
cross (John 19:30). He gave every evidence of dying. If Jesus
did not die, then He was not even a good person but a deceiver. But this is contrary to His unimpeachable moral character. We must also suppose that those standing around the
cross were deceived too, since they watched His suffering and
witnessed His death too. But it is implausible to assume that
everyone in the crowd, including the Roman soldiers, were
mistaken in what they saw and heard.

Third, the Roman soldiers pronounced Jesus dead (John
19:33, 34). Since they were accustomed to crucifixion and to
observing people die in this manner, it is unlikely that they
would have considered Jesus dead if He were not dead in fact.

Fourth, Pilate ordered his soldiers to check to make sure
Jesus was dead before he permitted Jesus to be buried (Mark
15:44-45). This double check adds further weight to the conclusion that Jesus really died.

Fifth, Jesus was embalmed and wrapped in nearly one hun-
dred pounds of material (John 19:40), which sealed Him in
His death shroud, and made any escape by the crucified
Jesus, had He been *only* human, virtually impossible.

Sixth, a heavy stone was rolled in front of the tomb and a
contingent of guards was placed there. Even if Jesus had not
died, but merely revived in the tomb, He could not have removed the stone, much less sneaked by the soldiers stationed
at the tomb's entrance.

Finally, even if Jesus had survived all this, His subsequent
appearances would have been more like a resuscitated wretch
than a triumphant Savior.

As even the liberal scholar, David Strauss, admitted:

It is impossible that a being who had stolen half-dead out of
the sepulchre, who crept about weak and ill, wanting medical

treatment, who required bandaging, strengthening and indulgence, and who still at last yielded his sufferings, could have given to his disciples the impressions that he was a conqueror over death, the prince of life, an impression which lay at the bottom of their ministry. Such a resuscitation could only have weakened the impression which he had made upon them in life and in death, at most could only have given it an elegiac voice, but could by no possibility have changed their sorrow into enthusiasm, have elevated their reverence into worship.[28]

Schonfield's *Passover Plot* Theory

Hugh J. Schonfield wrote a popular novel, *The Passover Plot* (1967),[29] that combines a number of features from various unorthodox views. He proposed that Jesus conspired with Joseph of Arimathea, Lazarus, and a young man to convince His disciples that He was the Messiah. This was to be done by manipulating events so that it looked like He fulfilled prophecy by taking drugs, feigning death, and reviving later. Unfortunately, the crucifixion wounds proved fatal. So the plotters had to dispose of Jesus' body, leaving the mystery of the empty tomb for the disciples. The appearances of Christ are explained as cases of mistaken identity.

Noted historian and archaeologist Dr. Edwin Yamauchi provided a definitive critique of the Passover Plot theory.[30] He notes the following serious problems. First, Schonfield assumes unfounded late dates for the New Testament books (mostly after A.D. 100). This is contrary to strong archaeological and manuscript evidence that places most New Testament books (including the Gospels) before A.D. 75.[31] Even the liberal scholar John A. T. Robinson dates the Gospels between A.D. 40 and 65.[32] This places them within the lifetimes of the eyewitnesses of the events—much too early for distortion of their witness without testable challenges from other contemporaries.

Second, it does not fit the high moral character of Christ to make Him into a clever messianic pretender. It makes Him out to be a cunning deceiver.

Third, it is highly implausible that Jesus could have hidden such a cunning plot from His closest friends and disciples. It is not only contrary to His known character but to the fact that the disciples, at least James, Peter, and John, were an intimate part of Jesus' life for years.

Fourth, there are many prophecies about the Messiah which Jesus could not have manipulated, including when (Dan. 9), where (Mic. 5:2), how (Isa. 7:14), and from what tribe (Gen. 49:19) and dynasty (2 Sam. 7) He would come. Nor is it plausible that Jesus could have staged or manipulated the reactions of others to Him, including John's heralding Him as King (Matt. 3), His accuser's reactions to Him (Matt. 27:12), the soldier's casting lots for His garments (John 19:23, 24), and that they would pierce His side (John 19:34). Fifth, it is highly improbable that anyone could have stolen the body from the heavily guarded tomb. As Matthew 28:12–15 indicates, the soldiers failure to guard the tomb would have resulted in severe discipline.

Sixth, the resurrection appearances cannot be cases of mistaken identity. There were too many people (over five hundred) who saw Jesus, on too many occasions (twelve), over too long a time (about forty days), with too much physical evidence of His identity and reality. They saw Him, heard Him, touched Him, saw His crucifixion wounds, observed the empty tomb and grave clothes, and ate with Him on at least four occasions (see Chapter 7).

There are, of course, other objections to the physical resurrection of Christ. The most important current one, that Jesus rose but not in historical space-time, will be discussed in the next chapter. This kind of denial is not part of classical liberalism but fits more with current neo-orthodox views of Christ.

Cultic Denials of the Resurrection

A Christian cult is a group that professes to be Christian yet denies one or more fundamental Christian teachings, such as the trinity, the deity or humanity of Christ, or His bodily resurrection. Of course, whether some unbiblical teaching qualifies as cultic will depend on precisely how the orthodox doctrine is defined. The teachings of the early Christian thinker Origen are a case in point.

Origen (A.D. 185–254)

The teachings of Origen and his followers were condemned on three occasions by Church Councils.[33] Origen was condemned for several teachings, most notably his universalism, an unbiblical belief that everyone is eventually going to be saved. However, at the root of Origen's doctrinal problem was his platonic tendency to spiritualize the literal truth of the Bible. He contended, for example, that the statement that Adam hid himself among the trees of the Garden, must be understood figuratively in Scripture, "that some mythical meaning may be indicated by it . . . ." In fact, he added, "the Gospels themselves are filled with the same kind of narratives; e.g., the devil leading Jesus up into a high mountain, in order to show him from thence the kingdoms of the whole world, and the glory of them."[34]

Origen also believed that eventually all beings would be "reconciled to God from a state of enmity." Thus when "all rational souls shall have been restored to a condition of this kind, then the nature of this body of ours will undergo a change into the glory of a spiritual body."[35] For Origen, universalism, and spiritualizing man's final state go hand in hand. His platonic tendencies led to his denial of the physical, material nature of the resurrection body.

Christ Had a Physical Body before the Resurrection

Origen was not a classic gnostic; he believed that Christ came in the flesh. Acknowledging the truth of John 1:14, Origen declared that "He [Jesus] became flesh, and having become flesh, 'He tabernacled among us . . . .' "[36] Further, he confessed that Jesus appeared in "human form, and announcing Himself as flesh, He calls to Himself those who are flesh . . . ."[37] Origen confessed the incarnation, the manifestation of Christ in a real physical, human body.

The Resurrection Transforms the Physical into the Spiritual

However, for Origen the resurrection of Christ marked a radical disjunction with the material, pre-resurrection body. He wrote:

> God created two general natures,—a visible, i.e., a corporeal nature; and an invisible nature, which is incorporeal . . . . But this corporeal nature admits of a change in substance; whence also God, the arranger of all things . . . [commands] that the corporeal nature may be *transmuted,* and *transformed* into any form of species whatever . . . (emphasis mine).[38]

Origen went on to say that "the whole of bodily nature will, in the consummation of all things, consist of one species, . . . the *spiritual body* (emphasis mine)."[39] The process by which this "different body" arrives is called transformation or transmutation. "Accordingly, it at one time puts off *one body* which was necessary before, but which is no longer adequate in its changed state, and it exchanges it for a *second* (emphasis mine)."[40] This new body will not be material or visible, for "those things 'which are seen are temporal, but those things which are not seen are eternal . . . .'" And "all those bodies which we see . . . and have been made with hands, but are not eternal, are far exceeded in glory by that which is not visible, nor made with hands, but is eternal."[41] Origen calls this body "spiritual," "celestial," and even "ethereal." He does not really believe in a resurrection of the physical body but in a qualitative transformation of it to an immaterial body.

The Post-Resurrection Body Was Immaterial

According to Origen, in the post-resurrection state, the believer "assumes another [body] in addition to the former, which is needed as a better covering, suited to purer ethereal regions of heaven."[42] He calls this a "spiritual body" and identifies it with the "house not made with hands, eternal in the heavens" of which Paul speaks in 2 Corinthians 5:1. Indeed, Origen says clearly:

We do *not* assert, however, that God will raise men from the dead with the same flesh and blood, as has been shown in previous pages; for we do not maintain that the natural body, which is sown in corruption, and in dishonour, and in weakness, will rise again as it was sown (emphasis mine).[43]

Origen adds, "We, therefore, do not maintain that the body which has undergone corruption resumes its original nature, any more than the grain of wheat which has decayed returns to its former condition."[44] Furthermore, "neither we, then, nor the holy Scriptures, assert that with the same bodies, without a change to higher condition, 'shall those who were long dead arise from the earth and live again;' for in so speaking, Celsus makes a false charge against us."[45] Origen cites in favor of his view Paul's statement in 1 Corinthians 15:49: "we shall also bear the image of the heavenly." But he believes that "the apostle wishes to conceal the secret meaning of this passage," thus necessitating that we take "a secret and mystical meaning."[46] It is with this mystical, platonic method of interpretation that he dematerialized the physical resurrection and spoke of an ethereal, spiritual body.

Jehovah's Witnesses

Jehovah's Witnesses also hold to an immaterial view of the nature of the resurrection body. This is evident throughout their writings.

Jesus Lived and Died in a Material Body

While they deny the deity of Christ, Jehovah's Witnesses do not deny that He possessed a real material human body. In fact, they believe He was *only* a man during His incarnation. They call his human body "the fleshly body . . . in which Jesus humbled himself, like a servant . . . ."[47] Jesus was "put to death in the flesh . . . ."[48] He was put in the grave as a "human creature."[49] They speak of "our Lord's human body, the one crucified . . . ."[50] So Jesus lived and died in a real human body of flesh and bones, a physical body.

Jesus Was Not Resurrected in His Body

However, Jehovah's Witnesses do not believe Christ rose in that same body that was placed in the tomb. Rather, it was an invisible, immaterial body.

> The fleshly body is the body in which Jesus humbled himself, like a servant, and is not the body of his glorification, nor the body in which he was resurrected.[51]
>
> So the King Christ Jesus was put to death in the flesh and was resurrected an invisible spirit creature.[52]
>
> The human body, the one crucified, was removed from the tomb by the power of God. . . . The Scriptures do not reveal what became of that body, except that it did not decay or corrupt.[53]
>
> Our Lord's human body . . . did not decay or corrupt. . . . Whether it was dissolved into gases or whether it is still preserved somewhere as the grand memorial of God's love, of Christ's obedience, and of our redemption, no one knows.[54]

In short, Jesus was not raised in the body in which He died. Rather, He rose in another body, one that was immaterial yet, like angels, capable of appearing in a different form.

Resurrection Appearances Are Only "Materializations"

According to Jehovah's Witnesses, Jesus' post-death appearances were simply His ability as a spirit to "materialize" for the purpose of communicating with His disciples.

> Therefore, the bodies in which Jesus manifested himself to his disciples after his resurrection were not the body in which he was nailed to the tree. They were merely materialized for the occasion, resembling on one or two occasions the body in which he died.[55]
>
> He [Christ] instantly created and assumed such a body of flesh and such clothing as he saw fit for the purpose intended.[56]

The New Age Denial of the Resurrection

The New Age writer of the *Aquarian Gospel of Jesus the Christ*,[57] Levi Dowling, also held to the immaterial nature of the resurrection body. He literally rewrote (allegedly through psychic powers) the life of Jesus in order to express his unorthodox view. In his account of the resurrection, the Jewish soldiers guarding the tomb heard a voice say, "Lord Christ arise," following which an angel tore the seal from the tomb. Then the soldiers "saw the body of the Nazarene transmute; they saw it change from mortal to immortal form, and then it disappeared" (XX. 172.39). Then, "they looked, the tomb was empty and the Lord had risen as he said" (XX. 172.42).

Later there was a "materialization of the spiritual body of Jesus" (XXI, title). These "materializations" were not visions. Dowling chides the disciples because they "thought they had seen a vision of the Lord. They did not think that he had risen from the dead." But Jesus appeared to them and said, "Behold, for human flesh can be transmuted into higher form, and then that higher form is master of things manifest, and can at will, take any form" (XXI. 173.27, 31).

On one occasion when Jesus was "fully materialized," he even showed his scars to some priests, saying, "Behold, for I am risen from the dead. Look at my hands, my feet, my side" (XXI. 176.11). Jesus explained to them what he had accomplished in his resurrection, declaring:

> The problem of the ages has been solved; a son of man has risen from the dead; he has shown that human flesh can be transmuted into flesh divine. Before the eyes of men this flesh in which I come to you was changed with the speed of light from human flesh. And so I am the message that I bring to you (XXI. 176.27–28).[57]

This process of "resurrection," or "transmutation," is described as that which "demonstrated unto us the power of man to rise from carnal flesh and blood to flesh of God . . ." (v. 3). Jesus was the first "master of the human race whose flesh has been transmuted into flesh divine." Thus the *Aquarian Gospel* concludes that "He is the God-man of to-day; but every one of earth shall overcome and be like him, a son of

God" (vv. 36–37). The Aquarian Jesus even went so far as to say,

> Behold my hands, my feet, my side and see the wounds the soldiers made. If you believe that I am phantom made of air, come forth and handle me; ghosts do not carry flesh and bones. I came to earth to demonstrate the resurrection of the dead, the transmutation of the flesh of carnal man to flesh of man divine" (XXI. 177.16–18).

The New Age Jesus explained his resurrection this way: "My human flesh was changed to higher form by love divine and I can manifest in flesh, or in the higher planes of life, at will." And "what I can do all men can do. Go preach the gospel of the omnipotence of man" (XXI. 178.13–14). This "resurrection" is described as being "quickened by the Holy Breath, [which] will raise the substance of the body to a higher tone, and make it like the substance of the bodies of the planes above, which human eyes cannot behold." This occurs when "God breathes, just as he breathed upon the chaos of the deep when worlds were formed, and life springs forth from death; the carnal form is changed to form divine." This is called a "deific life" (XXI. 178.36–42).

There is an obvious pantheistic context in which this concept of Jesus' "resurrection" is expressed, but there are also several strong similarities between this New Age idea and some unorthodox statements from Christians on the resurrection (see Chapter 6 for a thorough comparison). For instance, it confesses an empty tomb. The physical body that had lain there was "resurrected." It also confesses a physical or bodily resurrection, even calling it "divine flesh." In addition, it believes there were eye witnesses of the appearances of Christ after His resurrection. Furthermore, it even speaks of there being visible scars in the body that appeared after Jesus' resurrection.

Like other unorthodox statements on the resurrection, there are three crucial points to note here. According to Levi, the resurrection body is not the *same* body as the pre-resurrection body. It is a different body, composed of a different kind of substance, called "flesh of God."

Also, this resurrection body is essentially invisible and immaterial. It cannot be seen with the naked eye. The "appearances" of Jesus were not of the essential state of His resurrection body. They were merely "materializations" such as angels (who are spirits) did in the Bible.

Moreover, according to this unorthodox view, the resurrection did not occur in history. It was a super–historical event. Were someone to have witnessed the actual moment of the resurrection, all he would have seen would have been the corpse of Jesus vanish before his very eyes! The "resurrection" was really a transformation from a material state to an immaterial state. It was a movement from the visible, historical realm to the invisible, nonhistorical realm.

The Overwhelming Evidence

In summary, the overwhelming evidence is that Jesus physically died on the cross. Likewise, there is equally good testimony that He rose from the grave in that same physical body. The classic attempts to avoid this conclusion are without foundation. They are usually based on a faulty anti-supernaturalistic assumption that what happens only once is implausible, or on the unjustified assertion that the New Testament documents or witnesses are unreliable. This ignores the abundant evidence of thousands of manuscripts and the powerful testimony of over five hundred witnesses who saw, touched, handled, ate with, and were taught by Jesus for some forty days after His resurrection (see Chapter 7). Despite the counterclaims of the cults, it is inconceivable that the cloud of first century witnesses with all that time and all that tangible evidence were deceived about the physical nature of the resurrection of Christ. It is simpler just to heed the words of Jesus: "Look at my hands and my feet. It is I myself! Touch and see; a ghost does not have flesh and bone, as you see I have" (Luke 24:39 NIV)

6

Denials of the Physical Resurrection within the Church

"Indeed, nothing has been attacked with the same pernicious, contentious contradiction, in the Christian faith, as the resurrection of the flesh"————St. Augustine (*Psalms* 89, 32)

"There is nothing new under the sun." This adage seems to apply equally well to doctrinal deviations. The tendency to spiritualize Christian truths has been around since the first century. The apostle John warned against those who denied Jesus came in the flesh (1 John 4:2). Paul exhorted the Colossians to beware of an incipient gnosticism that claimed a deeper mystical knowledge (Col. 2:8ff.). In the second century this same tendency manifested itself in the platonic influence on eastern Christianity. This was most manifest in its tendency to allegorize Scripture, thereby denying the literal historical truth of many passages (see Chapter 5).

Today, the tendency to spiritualize is consistent with the denial of miracles as events in the world of space and time. Rather than events in real history, spiritualizers see miracles like the resurrection as events of "spiritual history" that have no observable or verifiable dimension.

Roman Catholic Denials: Edward Schillebeeckx

In his book *Jesus: An Experiment in Christology* (1979), the Roman Catholic theologian Edward Schillebeeckx argues that the resurrection of Christ was not in a physical, material body.[1] Strangely, he admits that there was an Old Testament (Dan. 12:1–3) and intertestamental (2 Bar. 49–51) belief "that the dead are to be raised in the condition of their former body, so that the living may see it is the dead who have been resurrected."[2] However, Schillebeeckx claims "the difference between the New Testament and late Jewish ideas of resurrection is immediately obvious." For "Jesus' resurrection is a saving event *per se*, not a condition for appearing alive before God's throne in order to be judged" (pp. 523, 524). Jesus' resurrection, then, is not a historical event; it is artificially dichotomized into a salvation event. And "the saving activity of God in raising Jesus from the dead does not lend itself easily to substantification" (p. 525). In other words, it's no good as an axillary to salvation if it's "real."

As a "saving event," the resurrection was not a visible event. Thus,

> the appearance is a salvific action of Jesus in the life of Peter and the Eleven; *ophthe*, Jesus "showed himself"; what is normally invisible was made to appear: that the invisible makes itself seen is expressed on lines of human perceiving, the human character of which is at the same time repudiated or corrected (p. 353).

The resurrection, for Schillebeeckx, is not physical but spiritual. It did not happen in space and time. Hence, the resurrection body was not empirically verifiable. According to Schillebeeckx it is like the "older non-apocalyptic books of the Old Testament [where] we hear of a resurrection that is a salvific event, but then in a spiritual sense (the 'resurrection of the people of Israel,' Isa. 26:19; 25:8)" (p. 524). This is why he believes that the "appearance" of Christ to Paul was not a physical appearance but a "conversion vision" that is "full of light symbols" derived from "a local Damascus tradition" (p. 369). However, in this kind of "Christ manifestation it is not necessary for one actually to see Jesus, in a visual sense" (p. 369).

As to the seemingly overwhelming New Testament evidence to the contrary (see Chapters 3, 8), Schillebeeckx simply responds, with absolutely no evidence to back him up: "In the oldest strata of the early Christian son of man tradition there is no explicit reference to resurrection, but there is reference to Jesus' being exalted to the presence of God and to his coming Parousia" (p. 537). For this reason the expression "on the third day" is not considered historical by Schillebeeckx. Rather, it "is charged with immense salvific implications. It tells us nothing about a chronological dating of the resurrection *qua* event (as, for instance, three days after Good Friday)" (p. 532).[3] Schillebeeckx's fatal flaw is that he *assumes* an irreconcilable inconsistency between "history" and "science" without a shred of logic or proof.

Neo-orthodox Views on the Resurrection: Rudolf Bultmann

It is common for neo-orthodox scholars to deny Jesus' resurrection in the flesh. Emil Brunner is a case in point. He declared emphatically:

Resurrection of the body, yes: Resurrection of the *flesh*, no! The "Resurrection of the body" does not mean the identity of the resurrection body with the material (although already transformed) body of flesh; but the resurrection of the body means continuity of the individual personality on this side, and on that, of death (emphasis mine).[4]

However, the most radical neo-orthodox influence on resurrection views comes from Rudolf Bultmann. Although he believed there was a historical Jesus of Nazareth, he denied the historicity of the resurrection. He concluded that the resurrection "is not an event of past history. . . . An historical fact which involves a resurrection from the dead is utterly inconceivable."[5] Why? First of all, there is "the incredibility of a mythical event like the resurrection of a corpse—for that is what resurrection means. . . ." Second, there is "the difficulty of establishing the objective historicity of the resurrection . . . ." Third, "the resurrection is an article of faith. . . . Fourth, "such a miracle is not otherwise unknown to mythology."[6] Bultmann has formed an unholy alliance between scientific antisupernaturalism and his own nebulous concept of spirit and myth.

What then is the resurrection, if not an event of space-time history? Bultmann replies: It is "abundantly clear that the New Testament is interested in the resurrection of Christ simply and solely because it is the eschatological event par excellence . . . ." Hence, "if the event of Easter Day is in any sense an historical event additional to the event of the cross, it is nothing else than the rise of faith in the risen Lord . . . ."[7] So "the historical problem is scarcely relevant to Christian belief in the Resurrection."[8] The resurrection is not an event of objective history. It is a "myth" which as such cannot be observed or verified. This from Bultmann, who knew Scripture well enough to know that it condemned the belief in myths (see, for example, 2 Peter 1:15–16).

Bultmann's objection to the historical nature of the resurrection can be summarized as follows:

1) Miracle stories ("myths") by nature are not historical.
2) The resurrection story is a miracle story.
3) Therefore, the resurrection is not an historical event.

In support of his contention, Bultmann points to the transcendent nature of a miracle. It is an "act of God." But God is beyond space-time history. His acts are transcendent; they are above observable human history. To reduce them to empirical history is to deny their transcendent, spiritual nature and to thereby rob them of their redemptive truth. Miracles are not of this world. They are acts in the spiritual world. In brief, Bultmann has defined them out of existence.

Aberrant Protestant Views on the Resurrection: Wolfhart Pannenberg

Although the German theologian Wolfhart Pannenberg confesses belief that Jesus left behind an empty tomb, he also denies that Jesus' resurrection was an historical event involving an observable body of flesh and bones. Rather, he views the "body" as spiritual or immaterial. Consider the following quotations:

The Resurrected Christ Left an Empty Tomb

Among the general historical arguments that speak for the trustworthiness of the report about the discovery of Jesus' empty tomb is, above all, the fact that the early Jewish polemic against the Christian message about Jesus' resurrection, traces of which have already been left in the Gospels, does not offer any suggestion that Jesus' grave had remained untouched.[9]

The Resurrected Christ Is Not Perceptible

Because the life of the resurrected Lord involves the reality of the new creation, the resurrected Lord is in fact not perceptible as one object among others in this world; therefore, he could only be experienced and designated by an extraordinary mode of experience, the vision, and only in metaphorical language (p. 99).

The Resurrected Christ Is Not Visible

With regard to the character and mode of the Easter appearances, the first thing to be considered is that it may have involved an extraordinary vision, not an event that was visible to everyone. This is especially clear with regard to the Damascus event (p. 93).

Resurrection Was in a Spiritual "Body"

Paul must have seen a spiritual body, a *soma pneumatikon*, on the road to Damascus, not a person with an earthly body (p. 92).

The Resurrection "Body" Is Not Corporeal

The appearances reported in the Gospels, which are not mentioned by Paul, have such a strongly legendary character that one can scarcely find a historical kernel of their own in them. Even the Gospel's reports that correspond to Paul's statements are heavily colored by legendary elements, particularly by the tendency toward underlining the corporeality of the appearances (p. 8).

The Resurrection "Body" Is Not One of Flesh

It is self-evident for him [Paul] that the future body will be a different one from the present body, not a fleshly body but—as he says—a "spiritual body" (p. 75).

There Is No Material Identity between Pre- and Post-Resurrected Christ

The transformation of the perishable into the spiritual body will be so radical that nothing will remain unchanged. There is no substantial or structural continuity from the old to the new existence (p. 76).

The Continuity Between the Pre- and Post-Resurrection Christ Is Historical, Not Material

Something different will be produced in its place, but there is a historical continuity in the sense of a continuous transition in the consummation of the transformation itself (p. 76).

So Pannenberg too denies the literal, material nature of the resurrection body, opting rather for an immaterial, spiritual body. It is not a body empirically observable in the space-time world

Aberrant Evangelical Views on the Resurrection

The platonic tendency to spiritualize is not limited to early church fathers like Origen, or even to more recent liberal scholars. What is alarming is that some evangelicals have embraced this view as well.

George Eldon Ladd

Professor Ladd of Fuller Seminary was one of the first American evangelicals to propound this unorthodox view of Jesus' resurrection. In his book, *I Believe in the Resurrection of Jesus*,[10] he denies all three of the historic orthodox characteristics of the resurrection: identity, materiality, and historicity.

Jesus' Pre- and Post-Resurrection Bodies Were Not Identical

Ladd claims that *"one* body is buried; *another* body springs forth" (p. 115). He adds, "during the forty days, he was in a different mode of existence which involved a different body . . ." (p. 127, emphasis mine). The continuity between the pre- and post-resurrection states of Jesus was personal, not material. According to Professor Ladd, "both Paul and the Gospels, though admittedly in different ways, describe the resurrection in terms of continuity of person and personality but *discontinuity* in the relationship of the resurrection body to the physical body" (p. 129, emphasis mine).

Jesus' Resurrection Body Is Invisible and Immaterial

According to Ladd, the resurrection body was by nature invisible and immaterial. For "Jesus was raised from the realm of mortal men into the unseen world of God" (p. 100). Ladd asks, "What would an observer have seen if he had stood inside the tomb watching the dead body of Jesus?" He answers, "All he would have seen was the sudden and inexplicable disappearance of the body of Jesus" (p. 100). What then did the disciples see if the risen Jesus was essentially invisible and immaterial? "They were momentary appearances of the invisible, risen Lord to the physical sight and senses of the disciples" (p. 100). The "appearances, then, were condescensions of the risen, exalted Lord by which he convinced his disciples that he was no longer dead" (p. 101). But the resurrection body was immaterial as such. For "at His resurrection he [Jesus] entered the invisible world of God" (p. 127). Thus, "His appearances to His disciples did not mean passing of one body through other solid substances; it means that Jesus, who was with them but invisible made himself visible to their physical senses" (p. 127).

Jesus' Resurrection Was Not Historical

According to Ladd, the resurrection was not an observable event in history, nor did the resurrected Christ become a part of the space-time universe. The resurrection "was not a re-

vivification of a dead corpse, returning to physical life"
(p. 94). Rather than reappearing in history, the resurrection
body, being invisible and immaterial, vanished from history.
Ladd wrote, "obviously the body had not been stolen. It had
simply disappeared" (p. 94). As such, the resurrection is not
historical. For "what does history or nature or the totality of
human experience know of any bodies which can pass
through solid rock? This is *historically* incredible" (p. 96, emphasis mine). To be sure, the resurrection was "an event in
which the world of God intersected the world of time and
space." And the appearances, when Jesus made his essentially
invisible nature visible for moments, were events in history
(pp. 100–101). However, "Christ in his resurrection entered
into a new realm of existence—a new order, which is nothing
less than the invisible world of God—the Age to Come"
(p. 117).

Furthermore, Ladd adds, "earthly, historical experience
knows nothing and has no analogy for what the New Testament says about the resurrection body" (p. 123). Hence, resurrection means "the radical transformation of the body of
Jesus from the world of nature to the world of God" (p. 125).
As Ronald Nash correctly notes, "Even though Ladd holds
that the resurrection was objective in the sense that it happened 'out there,' he stops short of allowing the resurrection
to be objective in the second sense, that is as a publicly observable event." Rather, "Ladd refuses to allow that the resurrection is verifiable in the same way that other historical
events are verifiable."[11] Resurrection is an event "in history"
only in the sense that the resurrection body by nature disappeared from observable history and from time to time it made
itself visible in the historical world. But neither the event of
the resurrection nor Jesus' continued appearances were empirically verifiable events in the space-time world.

E. Glenn Hinson

A recent example is that of Southern Baptist scholar
E. Glenn Hinson of Southern Seminary in Louisville. In his

book *Jesus Christ,* he argues that Jesus did not rise in the flesh but only in a spiritual body.

Jesus' Body before the Resurrection

Professor Hinson has no difficulty with the full humanity of Jesus. Jesus lived and died in human flesh.[12] Jesus was born, lived, ate, and slept like any other human being. In fact, His humanity is manifest in His mortality: "The most definite fact about Jesus is his crucifixion. No Christian, surely, could have invented a tale of the ignominious death of the founder of Christianity" (p. 97).

The Resurrection of Christ

While professor Hinson does not deny the reality of Jesus' physical death, he has serious doubts about the reality of His physical resurrection. "Although there is little debate that Jesus was crucified, there is much debate concerning the claim that he was raised from the dead" (p. 98). He rejects the "conservative Christian" belief that the resurrection is a historical fact and declares that "through the centuries the Church has wisely made the resurrection *an article of belief,* not a statement of fact" (p. 98, emphasis mine). For "to be [a] proven historical fact the resurrection would require extraordinary evidence because it is a unique, never before or since attested phenomenon" (p. 98). Hinson believes that "The fact that the resurrection was more than a historical event, a 'super-historical' event as it were, however, takes it beyond the historian's purview. It thus moves into the realm of faith" (p. 111).

What then was the resurrection? According to professor Hinson, it was not the "resurrection of the flesh." He rejects the view of those who

> wanted to view the resurrection in the crassest and most literal terms. Some at Corinth, for instance, expected an exact replica of the human form (see 1 Cor. 15:35–36), an expectation which undoubtedly derived from Jewish apocalyptic. That ex-

pectation recurred in the encounter with the docetists . . .
when the second century creed included belief in "resurrection of the *flesh*" (p. 111, emphasis mine).

Not only does Hinson reject the Jewish belief in a physical,
material resurrection, he also denies that it is a Greek view in
the immortality of the soul. Rather, "Paul was convinced that
the Christ who appeared to him belonged to another order of
existence than the Christ the disciples had known in the flesh.
The risen Christ has not a physical but a spiritual body" (p. 111,
emphasis mine).

Christ's Post-Resurrection Appearances

If Christ's post-resurrection body was not a physical body
of flesh, then what were His appearances to the disciples? According to Hinson, they were real "experiences" of the disciples, but not experiences of a real physical body. Rather,
Christ's appearances were like those of the angel of the
Lord—a visible manifestation of the invisible God. Hinson
concludes that "the appearances were more in the nature of
theophanies, like the Old Testament theophanies of Yahweh.
This would explain why, on the Emmaus road, for example,
the disciples failed to recognize Jesus until he did something
familiar to them" (p. 112).

Murray Harris

Another example is that of Murray Harris, a New Testament Professor at Trinity Evangelical Divinity School. His
denial of the material nature of the resurrection of Christ is
highly unusual for a professed evangelical. As such it deserves
special attention. A careful examination of Professor Harris's
writings on the resurrection reveal the same basic beliefs: 1)
Jesus had a physical, material body before the resurrection; 2)
At the moment of the resurrection this physical body was
changed into a body that is by nature an immaterial, spiritual
body; 3) Jesus' appearances after the resurrection were miraculous "materializations" of this essentially immaterial body
for evidential purposes (that is, in order to convince His disci-

ples of His reality, not of His materiality.) Let's examine his basic writings on the matter.

Raised Immortal (first published in 1983)[13] contains the basis for Harris' position concerning Christ's resurrection body.

First, Harris establishes that he believes Jesus' body was material before the resurrection. This view is not docetic. In contrast to the docetists (an early heretical group that denied the humanity of Christ), Harris believes that Jesus had a real, literal, human body. This body was material and spatial (p. 53).[14] It had physical characteristics (p. 121). It was visible and had an audible voice (pp. 46–47). It possessed physical (bodily) instincts (p. 124), was appropriately described as "flesh" (p. 132), and after the crucifixion lay as a corpse in the tomb (p. 133).

Second, *Raised Immortal* affirms Harris's unorthodox view that the resurrection changed Jesus' body into an immaterial body. Unlike Jehovah's Witnesses, Harris does not believe the physical body was changed into gases or preserved somewhere as a memorial. Rather, he believes that it underwent a "radical transformation" and was "changed into a spiritual mode of being" (p. 56). The resurrection body is no longer a body of "flesh" (p. 132). He says *"it will be neither fleshly nor fleshy"* (p. 124, emphasis mine).

The reasons given by Harris (from J. G. Davies) for explaining the illegitimacy of belief in the "resurrection of the flesh" are unconvincing. He lists: (1) "The influence of the idea that Christians will be raised like Christ (e.g., 1 Cor. 15:20)." (2) "The impact of millenarianism or chiliasm in the second century A.D. . . . has its corollary in a resurrection body suitable for life on earth." (3) An "Anti-Gnostic apologetic, which affirms the potential goodness of the flesh as being capable of salvation . . ." (4) "The partial acceptance in the early church of a Hellenistic anthropology that viewed man as divisible into corruptible body (flesh) and immortal soul" (p. 259).

The interesting thing about all of these factors is that, when stripped of the pejorative connotations, they are actually *arguments in favor of resurrection in the flesh*. For the Bible clearly teaches that we will be raised like Christ (see 1 Cor. 15:20; Phil. 3:21); that when Christ returns, the believing dead will "[come] to life and [reign] with Christ for a thousand years" (Rev. 20:6 NIV); that everything God made, including matter and flesh, is good (see Gen. 1:31); and that humans have both a material body and an immaterial soul that survives death (see Luke 23:43; Phil. 1:23; 2 Cor. 5:8; Rev. 6:9).

But on Harris's view, the believer's body, like Christ's, is altered at the moment of resurrection. "The physical body may be said to be transformed into a spiritual body or to be replaced by the spiritual body" (p. 127). Harris believes that this may be described as either a "metamorphosis" of the body or as an "exchange" of one body for another (p. 127). Thus, he speaks of "two forms of embodiment" (p. 126). That is, "one and the same person finds expression in two successive forms of embodiment—the physical and the spiritual . . ." (p. 126). It is for this reason that Harris concludes, "If, then, the notion of a material identity between the two forms of embodiment must be rejected, we may propose that the identity is personal" (p. 126). In other words, the same person is resurrected but in a "radically different" body (p. 128).

The disjunction between the material pre- and post-resurrection body is even more manifest in what Professor Harris says about the resurrection body of believers. He holds the highly unusual view that *believers receive their resurrection bodies at death, even though their physical bodies are still in the grave!* Harris concludes that "individual believers are resurrected at death" (p. 100). He bases this on 2 Corinthians 5, where Paul speaks of receiving a "heavenly dwelling" at the moment of death. This suggests "that between the destruction of the earthly house and the provision of the spiritual house there would be no 'interval of homelessness.'" Thus, "absent from the body and present with the Lord" (v. 8) means for Harris that we receive the resurrection body at the very moment of death (see Appendix E).

This unorthodox belief that Christians get their resurrection bodies even while their physical bodies are still in the grave reveals the radical discontinuity Harris sees between the pre- and post-resurrection bodies. Of course, in the case of Christ, Harris cannot deny the empty tomb. But even here the continuity between the pre- and post-resurrection Christ is not material, but only personal. The same Jesus arose, but not in the same material body. Rather than arising in a physical body of "flesh," Harris insists that it was radically transformed into an immaterial body. In his own words, the resurrection body is characterized by "essential immateriality" (p. 54).

In accordance with his belief that the resurrection body is by nature invisible and immaterial, Harris believes that the resurrection was a "trans–historical" event. It was "historical" or observable only when, like a theophany (see Appendix B), it occasionally materialized. "But it is not 'historical' in the sense of being an incident that was observed by witnesses or even an event that *could have been observed* by mortal gaze" (emphasis mine). Rather, "in his resurrected state Jesus was normally not visible to the human eye."[15] Therefore, "such a transaction clearly lies outside the scope of historical research; it is an item of faith."[16] Likewise, even Christ's ascension is only "*a parable* acted out for the benefit of the disciples as a visual and historical confirmation of *a spiritual reality . . .*" (p. 92, emphasis mine).

Third, Professor Harris asserts that Jesus' resurrection appearances were merely manifestations and not in the same physical body in which He died. Rather, they were in an "angel-like" body. That is, Christ's "appearances" were like theophanies (see Appendix B). Angels, however, are by nature spirits (see Heb. 1:14) who occasionally "materialize" so they can be seen (see Gen. 18, 19). Since Harris believes that the immaterial resurrection is "angel-like" (p. 123), it is not difficult to understand what he means by the appearances of Christ. He claims that they were *real*, but did not prove that the resurrection body was *material*. In his own words, one "characteristic of Jesus' resurrection body was *the ability to materialize and therefore be localized at will*" (p. 54). Jesus' purpose in His appearances or manifestations were apologetic in nature.

Harris contends that "what he [Jesus] wished them to understand *(idete)* by touching was not that he was material but that he was real . . ." (p. 54). Even Jesus eating "broiled fish" (Luke 24:42–43) is only a "parable acted out for the benefit of the disciples" (p. 92). Harris explains that "his [Jesus'] body was capable of receiving food for evidential reasons . . ." (p. 54).

Realizing the moral problem involved here, Harris adds unconvincingly, "In this accommodation to human understanding, Jesus was not party to deception. He took food to assure his disciples of his reality and to set them at their ease" (p. 54). Obviously there are ways for God or angels to assure us of their reality without acting out a "parable" of eating food. Spiritual beings have done it many times by mere visions or voices (see Gen. 22; Isa. 6; Matt. 1; Luke 1). It is clear from the context that Jesus was not simply attempting to prove to his disciples His *reality* but also His *materiality*.

Harris, would acknowledge that the resurrection and appearances happened in history, but would deny that the resurrection or the resurrection body were by nature observable, historical events. Harris says clearly:

> But it is not "historical" in the sense of being an incident that was observed by witnesses or even an incident that could have been observed by mortal gaze. We have already noted that there were no witnesses of the Resurrection itself and that in his resurrected state Jesus was normally not visible to the human eye.[17]

So by nature the resurrection body of Christ was not a visible part of objective history. In Harris's words, it is in this sense "trans-historical."[18]

Easter in Durham: Bishop Jenkins and the Resurrection of Jesus (1985)[19] is a booklet by Harris in which he expresses continued agreement with *Raised Immortal*, acknowledging that the latter "discusses in greater detail all the issues raised in this present essay." Indeed, an examination of the thirty-two page contents of *Easter in Durham* reveals the same basic beliefs.

First, it affirms that Jesus' Body before the Resurrection was material. The pre-resurrection body of Christ is called a "physical body." It is one "bound by material and spatial limitations" (p. 17). By nature it could be seen, heard, and handled. It was "crucified and placed in a tomb" (p. 14). Harris referred to it as "a buried corpse" (p. 16). In short, it was material like any other physical body in the space-time world.

Second, the resurrection altered the corpse into a spiritual body. As in his previous work, Harris believes that at the moment of the resurrection this previously material body underwent an "alteration" into a "spiritual body" (p. 17). This process is also called a "transformation" into "a spiritual mode of existence" (p. 17). It was a "metamorphosis" whose outcome was that "the same person occupied a different dwelling" (p. 20). Jesus was thereby "changed into a spiritual mode of existence" (p. 20). In this sense it was not a fresh "creation out of nothing," but it was a "different dwelling," and despite the personal identity there was "bodily discontinuity" (p. 20). So the tomb was emptied of the old material body, which was replaced by a new immaterial resurrection body.

Third, Harris distinguishes his view from others, pointing out Jesus' appearances were merely manifestations. Harris declares that in this new spiritual body Jesus' "essential state was one of invisibility and therefore immateriality. . . ." It "was not longer bound by material or spatial limitations. . . ." Jesus' immaterial resurrection body "could materialize and therefore be localized at will" (p. 17). But when Jesus appeared, it was for evidential reasons. These appearances or manifestations, like those of angels, could be seen, heard, and even touched (p. 24). However, they were not the "essential state" of the resurrection body, but merely an "occasional" manifestation in order to convince His disciples that He was real. They were not the natural state of the resurrection body, but were "miraculous occurrences that pointed beyond themselves to spiritual truths about Jesus" (p. 17).

Since the booklet is written as a refutation of a liberal Bishop who believed the resurrection appearances were only subjective experiences of the disciples, there is understandably a greater emphasis here on the reality of Christ's resurrection and post-resurrection appearances. However, there is no perceptible or confessed change of view from his earlier work *(Raised Immortal)*, which was republished (by Eerdmans) without change of view the very same year he wrote *Easter in Durham* (1985). In both books the resurrection of Christ is presented as not being in the flesh but in an immaterial body.

"Raised . . . Never to Die Again" (1988) is an article put out more recently by Professor Harris in *Voices* (June, 1988),[20] published by Trinity Evangelical Divinity School. Although the emphasis is somewhat different and the presentation more popular (for a lay audience), the same three elements of his view are expressed here as well. Even though this tiny article is barely over one page, it contains the following:

1) Jesus' body before the resurrection was material. Again, there is no denial of a normal, physical pre-resurrection body of Jesus. Like other material bodies it could (and did) experience "death" (p. 13). It was also placed in a "burial-cave" (p. 13). In this and all other respects Jesus' pre-resurrection body was no different from any other physical body.

2) Resurrection changed Jesus' body into an immaterial body. The moment of Jesus' resurrection produced a body that was "radically different" (p. 12). Unlike His previous physical body, the resurrection body was an immaterial or "glorious body" (p. 13). It was "so different" from His physical pre-resurrection body that it was in fact "unique" (p. 12). As a result it was not a "normal life" (p. 13). Nor was it simply a "reanimation," "renewal," or "resuscitation" (p. 13), but it was a "resurrection to immortality" (p. 12).

3) The appearances of Christ after His resurrection are not mentioned. In this two-page article there are no references to post-resurrection appearances, although there is one to John's

vision in Revelation 1. Neither is there any indication of Harris's change of view from his previous writings, where Jesus' post-resurrection appearances were described as "materializations" for the purpose of convincing His disciples of His reality and victory over death.[21]

Some have concluded mistakenly that Professor Harris has changed his views on the nature of the resurrection body. This conclusion is based on a published letter from Professor Harris to Dr. Kenneth Meyer, president of Trinity Evangelical Divinity School.[22] Professor Murray Harris made the following statement:

> I am happy to reaffirm that I believe that our Lord rose from the dead in the actual, physical body he possessed before his death but that as a result of his resurrection there was an alteration and enhancement of the properties of that physical body so that he now possesses what Paul calls a "spiritual body" (1 Cor. 15:44–49) or a "glorious body" (Phil. 3:21). Before the resurrection, the body of Jesus was mortal (Mark 15:37; Col. 1:22); through the resurrection, the body of Jesus became immortal (Rom. 6:9; Heb. 7:16; Rev. 1:18).

However, this letter signals no real change of view for several reasons.

First, he says nothing new here but claims merely to "reaffirm" what he already believed, which is a clear denial of the literal, material nature of the resurrection body.

Second, in response to my question, "Do you now believe that Christ's resurrection body was a literal, physical body?", Professor Harris answered explicitly by letter to me on November 17, 1987: "My view about the resurrection of Jesus has never changed."

Further, nearly eight months after he wrote the letter of June 17, 1988 (cited above), he still claimed to hold the same view on the nature of the resurrection body. In response to the question, "Do these articles reflect a change in view . . . ?", he replied, "I believe that my written statements and oral affirmations about the nature of Christ's resurrection body have always been consistent with one another."[23]

firmations about the nature of Christ's resurrection body have always been consistent with one another."[23]

Third, it is not clear whether in Harris's letter the phrase "actual, physical body" should be understood to refer to Jesus' body after it was raised or only to the one "he possessed before his death."

Fourth, even if "physical" is meant to apply to the nature of the resurrection body, it is clear that it does *not* mean a material body of flesh. Indeed, he says just the opposite here, namely, Jesus' physical, material body underwent an "alteration" into a "spiritual body." This is in accord with what he has always held: the resurrection body is by nature "invisible" and "immaterial."

Fifth, there is an ambiguity in the word "actual." Even if "*actual*, physical body" refers to the nature of the resurrection body, it is not the equivalent of saying that Jesus' resurrection body was the "*same* physical body" as His pre-resurrection body. In fact, without changing his view, Harris cannot affirm consistently that the resurrection body is the *same* physical, material body, since he affirms that it is a "radically different" body. He even refers to the pre- and post-resurrection states as "two successive but different types of body." He says clearly it is a "numerically different" body (see quotes above).

In brief, his letter to Dr. Meyer contains the same elements of his previously stated views—namely, (1) Jesus had a "physical" and "mortal" body before His resurrection, (2) but the resurrection "altered" His physical body into a totally different kind of body, namely a "spiritual" or immaterial body, (3) and, hence, the appearances of Christ after the resurrection were merely to convince His disciples of His *reality*, not of His *materiality*.

Common Elements in Unorthodox Views

Despite their differences, the unorthodox views of Jesus' resurrection generally have three common elements. They *deny* the resurrection's

> materiality,
> numerical identity,
> and historicity.

However, as we have seen in Chapters 1–4, these three elements are at the heart of the orthodox view of the resurrection. Therefore, these views are unorthodox on all three counts. Of course, they do acknowledge the orthodox belief in the immortality of the resurrected Christ. But without an immortal material body, this view differs little from the Greek concept of an immortal spiritual entity. Certainly, if Paul had preached to Greeks on Mars Hill that believers were raised in an invisible, immaterial form while their physical bodies were still in the grave, his listeners would not have mocked him (see Acts 17:32). This view would not have been substantially different from their own belief in the immortality of the immaterial person.

The three characteristics generally present in these current denials of the orthodox view on the resurrection stand in stark contrast to the historic, biblical position.

They claim that Jesus was resurrected in a *numerically different* body from the one in which He died. It was not numerically the same body; it had no material continuity with the first one. Some, like professor Murray Harris, even go so far as to say that believers receive their new resurrection bodies at death, while their material bodies are obviously still in the graves.

Unlike the orthodox view, they also claim that the resurrection body was by nature *immaterial and invisible*. Its essence was "spiritual" and "angel-like." As an invisible body, it could not be seen as such by the naked eye, except when it "materialized" for the purpose of communicating with the visible world. Hence, in contrast to the orthodox position, they also deny that Christ was raised in the *flesh*. For them, the resurrection triumphs over the flesh by the spirit, resulting in a body that is spiritual by nature, not material.

Another characteristic of this deviant stand on the resurrection is its contention that the resurrection is *not historical* but is super-historical—it did not occur in humanly observable space and time. In other words, the resurrection body cannot be observed as part of the empirical world; it is part of salvation history, but not by nature a part of regular, observable history.

**RESURRECTION: HISTORICAL/
SUPER-HISTORICAL**

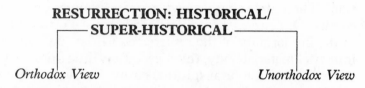

	Orthodox View	*Unorthodox View*
Super-Historical Aspects	Who? *God* Why? *Salvation* Beyond	Who? *God* Why? *Salvation* What? *Spiritual life* Where? *Spiritual world* Space & Time
Historical Aspects	Within What? *Physical life* Where? *Physical world*	Space & Time

From this it is clear that the crucial difference in the views is not whether there are super-historical aspects of the resurrection. Both views agree on the *source* (God). Both agree that there is a super-historical *significance* to the resurrection, namely, salvation. But the crucial difference is about the *sphere* of resurrection.

The unorthodox view denies that the resurrection of Christ is in essence a *historical* event. They deny that Jesus was raised in the *same* visible *material* body that was part of the space-time world. In this vital sense they are all denials of the orthodox view of the bodily resurrection of Christ.

Until recently, few professed evangelicals have ventured to deny any of these three essentials of the orthodox understanding of the resurrection. Now some deny all of them. To be sure, some are more radical than others, but all deny that

Jesus was resurrected in the same observable, material body in which He was crucified. The differences in the views have to do with whether the tomb was empty; whether Jesus actually appeared to His disciples in a new (immaterial) body that could be touched. The similarities and differences can be shematized as follows:

UNORTHODOX VIEWS

Common elements: (held by all)	1. Not Numerically Identical 2. Not a Material Body 3. Not a Historical Event		
Differences:	Bultmann	Pannenberg	Harris/Ladd
Empty Tomb	no	yes	yes
Appearances	no	no	yes

The intramural differences in the unorthodox views have to do with the empty tomb and the post-resurrection experiences. Bultmann is the most radical, denying any objective reality to them altogether. Harris is the least radical advocate of the unorthodox positions, admitting that there was an empty tomb and that the immaterial, resurrected Christ "materialized" on occasions and was seen by the disciples. However, *all* these unorthodox views have three key elements in common:

1) It was *not numerically identical* with the pre-resurrection body.
2) Jesus' resurrection body was *not material.*
3) The resurrection body was not by nature a *historically observable object.*

In brief, these current views deny all three elements in the orthodox view of the physical nature of the resurrection—*numerical identity, materiality, and historicity.* But the resurrection is a kingpin of the Christian faith. Therefore, we will examine carefully in the next chapters the reasons for this current denial of the orthodox view of the resurrection.

7

Physical Resurrection vs. Immaterial Resurrection

The battle for the resurrection has changed its front. Once it was a battle against liberals who denied the physical resurrection (see Chapter 5). Now it is a battle with evangelicals who deny the physical nature of the resurrection body.

There are three centers of concern in this debate. First, it is no longer a battle over whether a body rose from the tomb, but whether it was the *same physical body* that was placed there. Second, it is no longer a fight about the reality of the resurrection, but about its *materiality*. Third, it is not a question of the actuality of the resurrection, but of its *historicity*.

The seriousness of the resurrection crisis confronting the Christian church can be appreciated by identifying several arguments used by these unorthodox evangelicals to deny that Christ rose in the same physical, material body which was crucified and placed in the tomb.

Paul Speaks of a "Spiritual Body"

In 1 Corinthians 15:44 Paul refers to the resurrection body as a "spiritual body," in contrast to the pre-resurrection body, which in the same verse is described as "natural body." The unorthodox view assumes that a spiritual body is immaterial and invisible. But a study of the context does not support this conclusion for several reasons.

"Spiritual" Means Immortal, Not Immaterial

A "spiritual" body denotes an immortal one, not an immaterial one. A "spiritual" body is one dominated by the spirit, not one devoid of matter. The Greek word *pneumatikos* (translated "spiritual" here) means a body directed by the spirit, as opposed to one under the dominion of the flesh. It is not ruled by flesh that perishes but by the spirit that endures (vv. 50–58). So "spiritual body" here does not mean immaterial and invisible but instead immortal and imperishable.[1]

"Spiritual" Denotes a Supernatural Body

Further, the resurrection body Paul referred to here is supernatural. The series of contrasts used by Paul in this passage reveals that the resurrection body was a supernatural body. While it is still physical, it is also immortal.

PRE-RESURRECTION BODY	POST-RESURRECTION BODY
Earthly (v. 40)	Heavenly
Perishable (v. 42)	Imperishable
Weak (v. 43)	Powerful
Mortal (v. 53)	Immortal
Natural (v. 44)	[Supernatural]

The complete context indicates that "spiritual" *(pneumatikos)* could be translated "supernatural" in contrast to "natural." This is made clear by the antithetical parallels of perishable and imperishable, corruptible and incorruptible, etc.

In fact, this same Greek word *pneumatikos* is translated "supernatural" in 1 Corinthians 10:4, speaking of the "supernatural rock that followed them in the wilderness" (RSV). The *Greek-English Lexicon of the New Testament* says, "That which belongs to the supernatural order of being is described as *pneumatikos:* accordingly, the resurrection body is a *soma pneumatikon* [supernatural body]."[2]

"Spiritual" Refers to Material Objects

Sometimes the word "spiritual" refers to material objects. A study of Paul's use of the same word "spiritual" in other passages reveals that it does not refer to something that is purely immaterial. First of all, Paul spoke of the "spiritual rock" that followed Israel in the wilderness, from which they got "spiritual drink" (1 Cor. 10:4). But the Old Testament story (Exod. 17; Num. 20) reveals that it was a physical rock from which they got literal water to drink. The *actual* water they drank from that *material* rock was produced *supernaturally*. Hence, the Revised Standard Version properly translates the Corinthian passage as follows:

> All ate the same supernatural food and all drank the same supernatural drink. For they drank from the supernatural Rock which followed them, and the Rock was Christ (1 Cor. 10:3-4).

That is to say, the supernatural Christ was the source of these supernatural manifestations of natural food and water. Just because the physical provisions came from a spiritual (that is, supernatural) source did not make the provisions themselves immaterial. When Jesus supernaturally made bread for the five thousand (John 6), He made literal bread. However, this literal, material bread could have been called "spiritual" bread because of its supernatural source, in the same way that the literal manna given to Israel is called "spiritual food" (1 Cor. 10:4).[3]

Further, when Paul spoke about a "spiritual man" (1 Cor. 2:15), he obviously did not mean an invisible, immaterial man with no corporeal body. He was, as a matter of fact, speaking of a flesh-and-blood human being whose life was empowered by the supernatural power of God. He was referring to a literal person whose life had spiritual direction. A spiritual man is one who is taught by the Spirit and who ac cepts the things that come from the Spirit of God (1 Cor. 2:13-14). The resurrection body can be called a "spiritual body" in much the same way we speak of the Bible as a "spiritual book." Regardless of their spiritual source and power, both the resurrection body and the Bible are material objects.

The New International Dictionary of New Testament Theology says that "spiritual" is used "in contrast to the *merely* material or to those activities, attitudes, etc. which derive from the flesh and draw their significance from the *merely* physical, human and worldly" (emphasis mine).[4]

"Spiritual" does not necessarily mean something purely immaterial or intangible. The spiritual man, like the spiritual rock and spiritual food, was physical, but was acted upon by spiritual or supernatural power.

The Emphasis on Christ's Ability to Appear

Some argue that the resurrection body was essentially immaterial and invisible and, therefore, not an object observable or testable by empirical or sensory means. The resurrection appearances are inherently nonhistorical. The New Testament stresses the fact that it could appear,[5] they argue, thus implying that it was invisible other than when it appeared (see Luke 24:34; Acts 9:17; 13:31; 26:16; 1 Cor. 15:5-8). Each of these times, they say, "he appeared" or "he let himself be seen" (aorist passive). Grammatically, the action rests on the one who appears, not on the one who sees Him appear. This, they argue, implies that Jesus was essentially invisible, and materialized during the occasions of His resurrection appearances. However, this argument fails for several reasons.

Christ's Resurrection Body Could Be Seen

During Christ's appearances He could be seen with the naked eye. His appearances could be tested by sight. They are described by the word *horao* ("to see"). Although this word is sometimes used of seeing invisible realities (Luke 1:22; 24:23), it often means to see by the naked eye.[6] For example, John uses the same word *horao* for seeing Jesus in His earthly body before the resurrection (John 6:36; 14:9; 19:35) and also of seeing Him in His resurrection body (20:18, 25, 29). Since the same word for body *soma* is used of Jesus before and after the resurrection (1 Cor. 15:44; Phil. 3:21), and since the same word for its appearing *horao* is used of both, there is no reason for believing the resurrection body is not the same literal, material body.

The phrase "he let himself be seen"[7] (aorist passive, *ophthe*), means that Jesus took the initiative to *show* Himself to the disciples, not to materialize a body for their benefit. The same form ("He [they] appeared") is used in the Greek Old Testament (see 2 Chron. 25:21), in the Apocrypha (see 1 Macc. 4:6),[8] and in the New Testament (see Acts 7:26) of human beings appearing in physical, material bodies. In this passive form the word means to initiate an appearance for public view, to move from a place where one is not seen to a place where one is seen. It does not necessarily mean that what is by nature invisible becomes visible.[9] Rather, it means more generally "to come into view." There is no necessity to understand it as referring to something invisible by nature becoming visible, as Harris does. [10] In that case it would mean that these human beings in normal pre-resurrection bodies were essentially invisible before they were seen by others.

Furthermore, the same event that is described by "he appeared" or "let himself be seen" (aorist passive), such as the appearance to Paul (1 Cor. 15:8), is also described in the active mood. That is, the appearance is described by the viewer himself. Paul wrote of this same experience in the same book, "Have I not seen Jesus Christ our Lord?" (1 Cor. 9:1 NKJV).

Christ's Appearances Were "Natural"

The word "appeared" *(ophthe)* refers to a natural event. This is supported by several lines of evidence. First, Arndt and Gingrich's *Greek-English Lexicon of the New Testament* points out that the word is used "of persons who appear in a natural way."[11] *The Theological Dictionary of the New Testament* notes that appearances "occur in a reality which can be perceived by the natural senses."[12] In his *Linguistic Key to the New*

Testament, Fritz Rienecker notes that "appeared" means "He could be seen by human eyes, the appearances were not just visions (Grosheide)."[13]

Second, the visual *apprehension* of Jesus' resurrection body was not a miracle, but the *way* in which it often appeared was miraculous. The gospels say that Jesus appeared *suddenly*. They also assert that Jesus could disappear suddenly. Luke writes of the two disciples on the road to Emmaus, "Then their eyes were opened, and they knew Him; and He *vanished* from their sight" (Luke 24:31 NKJV, emphasis mine). Jesus also disappeared from the disciples on other occasions (Luke 24:51; Acts 1:9). Evangelicals who depart from the orthodox doctrine of the resurrection argue that His ability to appear suddenly can be taken as evidence that His resurrection body was essentially invisible. But by the same reasoning, His ability to disappear suddenly could be used as evidence that His body was essentially *material* and could suddenly become *immaterial*.

Third, there are much more reasonable explanations for the biblical stress on Christ's self-initiated "appearances." They were not designed to imply that His resurrection body was immaterial. Rather they were designed to prove his triumph over death of the physical body.

First of all, they were proof that He had conquered death (Acts 13:30–31; 17:31; Rom. 1:4). Jesus said, "I am the Living One; I was dead, and behold I am alive for ever and ever! And I hold the keys of death and Hades" (Rev. 1:18; compare John 10:18 NIV). The translation "he let himself be seen" is a perfectly fitting way to express this self-initiated triumphalism. He was sovereign over death as well as His resurrection appearances.

Furthermore, no human being saw the actual moment of the resurrection. But the fact that Jesus appeared repeatedly in the same body for some forty days (Acts 1:3) to over five hundred different people (1 Cor. 15:6) on twelve different occasions is indisputable evidence that He really rose from the dead in the same physical body. In brief, the reason for the stress on the many appearances of Christ is not because the resurrection body was essentially invisible and immaterial, but rather to show that it was actually material and immortal. Without an empty tomb and repeated appearances of the same material body that was once buried in it, there would be no proof of the resurrection.

It is not surprising at all that the Bible stresses the many appearances of Christ. They are the proof of the physical resurrection.

Resurrection Appearances Are Called Visions

The contention that resurrection appearances are called visions is also used to support the immaterial view of the resurrection body.[14] Luke records that women at the tomb "had seen a vision of angels, who said he was alive" (Luke 24:23 NIV). But, they argue, visions are always of invisible, unseen realities, not of physical, material objects. The miracle is that these spiritual realities can be seen. A spiritual body is angel-like and, therefore, cannot be seen. In addition, some point to the fact that those who were with Paul during his Damascus road experience did not see Christ.[15] They call his experience of the resurrected Christ a vision. But this reasoning seems to be flawed.

The Resurrection Is Not Called a Vision

The passage cited above from Luke 24:23 does not say that seeing the resurrected Christ was a vision; it refers only to seeing the angels at the tomb as a vision. The Gospels never speak of a resurrection appearance of Christ as a vision, nor does Paul in his list of appearances in 1 Corinthians 15.

The only possible reference to a resurrection appearance as a vision is in Acts 26:19 where Paul says: "I was not disobedient to the heavenly vision." But even if this is a reference to the Damascus appearance of Christ, it is merely an overlap in usage of the words. For Paul clearly calls this event an "appearance" (1 Cor. 15:8) in which he had "seen Jesus our Lord" and, hence, was given apostolic credentials (see 1 Cor. 9:1; compare Acts 1:22).

However, it is possible that even in Acts 26:19 the word "vision" refers to the subsequent revelation to Ananias through whom God gave Paul's commission to minister to the Gentiles (Acts 9:10–19). This interpretation can be supported by several factors. First, Paul says nothing about seeing the Lord in this passage (Acts 26:19), as he does when referring to his Damascus experience (Acts 22:8; 26:15). Second, when having a "vision" *(optasia)* Paul clearly designates it as such (see 2 Cor. 12:1) in distinction from a real appearance. Third, Paul did not receive his specific missionary mandate from his Damascus road experience (Acts 9:1–9). Rather, he was told "to go into the city, and you will be told what you must do" (v. 5). Fourth, it was there in the city through a "vision" (v. 10) to Ananias that Paul was given his missionary mandate "to carry my [Christ's] name before the Gentiles" (9:15 NIV). Fifth, Ananias's reference to Paul's "vision" may not have been to the Damascus road physical appearance of Christ to Paul but to a later vision he got while "praying in the house of Judas on Strait Street in Damascus" (Acts 9:11–12 NIV). It was here that he was told specifically that Ananias would lay hands on him (v. 12). So when Paul said "I was not disobedient to the heavenly vision" (Acts 26:19 NIV), it was to the mandate through Ananias's vision that Paul refers. Sixth, the word "vision" *(optasia)* is never used of a resurrection appearance anywhere in the Gospels or Epistles. It is always used of a purely visionary experience (Luke 1:22; 24:23; 2 Cor. 12:1).

Whatever the case, the *Theological Dictionary of the New Testament* correctly notes about visions that the New Testament "distinguish[es] them from the Damascus experience."[16]

Appearances Are Different from Visions

The post-resurrection encounters with Christ are consistently described as literal "appearances" (see 1 Cor. 15:5–8), not as visions. The difference between a mere vision and a physical appearance is significant. Visions are of invisible, spiritual realities, such as God and angels. Appearances, on the other hand, are of physical objects that can be seen with the naked eye. Visions have no physical manifestations associated with them, but appearances do.

People sometimes "see" or "hear" things in their visions (see Luke 1:11f.; Acts 10:9f.) but not with their physical eyes or ears. When someone saw angels with the naked eye or had some physical contact with them (see Gen. 18:8; 32:24; Dan. 8:18), it was not a vision but an actual appearance of the angel in the physical world. During these appearances, the angels temporarily assumed a visible form, after which they returned to their normal invisible state. However, the resurrection appearances of Christ were experiences of seeing Christ in His continued visible, physical form with the naked eye. Thus, there is a significant difference between a vision and a physical appearance.

VISION	APPEARANCE
Of a Spiritual Reality	Of a Physical Object
No Physical[17] Manifestations	Physical Manifestations
Daniel 2, 7	1 Corinthians 15
2 Corinthians 12	Acts 9

Certainly the most common way to describe an encounter with the resurrected Christ in Scripture is as an "appearance." These appearances were accompanied by physical manifestations such as the audible voice of Jesus, His physical body and crucifixion scars, physical sensations (touch), and eating on four occasions. These phenomena are not purely subjective or internal; they involve a physical, external reality.

Moreover, the contention that Paul's experience must have been a vision because those with him did not see Christ is unfounded for several reasons. First of all, Paul lists this as a physical appearance just like those seen by the other apostles immediately after the resurrection (1 Cor. 15:6). Second, unlike a vision, this appearance had physical phenomena associated with it, such as sound and light. Third, those who were with Him experienced the same physical phenomena. The

Bible says, "they heard[18] the sound . . ." (Acts 9:7) and "saw the light" (Acts 22:9). The fact that they "did not see any-one" (Acts 9:7 NIV) is not surprising since even Paul was physically blinded by the brightness of the light they all saw (vv. 8–9). Apparently only Paul looked straight into the light. Hence, only he actually saw Christ, and only he was literally stricken blind by it (Acts 22:11; 26:13). Hence it was an expe-rience of a real physical reality. Those who were with Paul saw and heard it with their natural eyes and ears.

Christ Was Sovereign over His Appearances

These critics also argue that Jesus' sovereignty over His appearances indicates that He was essentially invisible, and made Himself visible only when He wished to do so. In this connection they note that Jesus did not appear to unbelievers, supposedly indicating that He was not naturally visible to the naked eye. However, this conclusion is unwarranted.

Jesus Did Appear to Unbelievers

It is incorrect to say that Jesus did not appear to unbeliev-ers. In fact, He appeared to the most hostile unbeliever of all, Saul of Tarsus (Acts 9:1ff.). As far as His resurrection is con-cerned, even His disciples were at first unbelievers. When Mary Magdalene and others reported that Jesus was resur-rected "they did not believe the women, because their words seemed to them like nonsense" (Luke 24:11 NIV). Later Jesus had to chide the two disciples on the road to Emmaus about disbelief in His resurrection, "How foolish you are, and how slow of heart to believe all that the prophets have spoken!" (Luke 24:25 NIV). Even after Jesus appeared to the women, to Peter, to the two disciples and to the ten apostles, still Thomas said, "Unless I see the nail marks in his hands and put my finger where the nails were, and put my hand into his side, I will not believe it" (John 20:25 NIV).

In addition to appearing to His unbelieving disciples, Jesus also appeared to some who were not His disciples at all. He appeared to His unbelieving brothers (see John 7:5). He appeared to his brother James (1 Cor. 15:7) and probably also to Jude (v. 1), as well as to the unbelieving Saul of Tarsus (Acts 9). Thus, it is false to claim that Jesus did not appear to unbelievers.

Selectivity Does Not Prove Invisibility

The fact that Jesus was selective about those He wanted to see Him does not indicate that He was essentially invisible. Jesus was also in control of those who wanted to lay hands on Him before the resurrection. On one occasion an unbelieving crowd tried to take Jesus and "throw him down a cliff. But he walked right through the crowd and went on his way" (Luke 4:30 NIV; compare John 8:59; 10:39).

Even before His resurrection, Jesus was also selective about those for whom He performed miracles. He refused to perform miracles in His own home area "because of their lack of faith" (Matt. 13:58). Jesus even disappointed Herod, who had hoped to see Him perform a miracle (Luke 23:8). The truth is that Jesus refused to cast "pearls before swine" (Matt. 7:6). In submission to the Father's will (John 5:30), He was sovereign over His activities both before and after His resurrection. This in no way proves that He was essentially invisible and immaterial either before or after His resurrection.

Jesus Could Get Inside Closed Rooms

Some infer that since the resurrected Christ could appear in a room with closed doors (John 20:19), His body must have been essentially immaterial. Others suggest that He materialized and dematerialized on this occasion. But such conclusions are not warranted.

The text does not actually say Jesus passed through a closed door. It simply says that "when the disciples were together, with the doors locked for fear of the Jews, Jesus came and stood among them" (John 20:19 NIV). The text does not say how He got into the room.[19]

If He had chosen to pass through closed doors, Jesus could

have performed this same miracle before His resurrection with His unglorified material body. As the Son of God, His miraculous powers were just as great before the resurrection as they were after it.

Even before His resurrection Jesus performed miracles with His physical body that transcended natural laws, such as walking on water (John 6:16–20). Walking on water did not prove that His pre-resurrection body was immaterial, or even that it could dematerialize (see Appendix F). Otherwise, Peter's pre-resurrection walk on water would mean his body dematerialized for a moment and then quickly rematerialized (Matt. 14:29)!

Although physical, the resurrection body is by its very nature a supernatural body. It should be expected that it can do supernatural things like appearing in a room with closed doors.

Further, according to modern physics, it is not an impossibility for a material object to pass through a door; it is only statistically improbable. Physical objects are mostly empty space. All that is necessary for one physical object to pass through another is for the right alignment of the particles in the two physical objects. This is no problem for the One who created the body to begin with.

Jesus Appeared and Disappeared Instantaneously

Some argue that Jesus' ability to appear and disappear immediately was proof of the immaterial nature of the resurrection body (Luke 24:36). This reasoning overlooks several facts.

One is that this argument fails to recognize that while the resurrection body as such has *more* powers than a pre-resurrection body, it is not *less* physical. That is, it does not cease to be a material body, even though by resurrection it gains powers beyond mere physical bodies.

Additionally, it is the very nature of a miracle that it is immediate, as opposed to a gradual natural process. When Jesus touched the man's hand, *"immediately* he was cured" (Matt. 8:3 NIV, emphasis mine). At Jesus' command the paralytic rose up *immediately,* took up his pallet and went out in the sight of all (Mark 2:10–12). When Peter proclaimed cured the man born crippled, *"instantly* the man's feet and ankles became strong. He jumped to his feet and began to walk" (Acts 3:7 NIV, emphasis mine).

Moreover, Philip was immediately transported from the presence of the Ethiopian eunuch in his physical pre-resurrection body. The text says that after baptizing the eunuch "the Spirit of the Lord *suddenly* took Philip away, and the eunuch did not see him again . . ." (Acts 8:39 NIV, emphasis mine). One moment Philip was with the eunuch; the next he suddenly and miraculously disappeared and later appeared in another city (Acts 8:40). Such phenomenon does not necessitate an immaterial body. Sudden appearances and disappearances are not proofs of the immaterial but of the supernatural.

The Elements of the Physical Body Decay

Some have argued in favor of an immaterial resurrection body on the grounds used by the old Socinian that a physical resurrection body would imply "a crassly materialistic view of resurrection according to which the scattered fragments of decomposed corpses were to be reassembled. . . ."[20] This objection is unconvincing for a number of reasons.

It is unnecessary to the orthodox view to believe that the same before-death particles will be restored in the resurrection body (see Appendix A). Even common sense dictates that a body can be the same physical body without having the same physical particles. The observable fact that bodies eat food and give off waste products, as well as get fatter and skinnier, is sufficient evidence of this. Certainly, we do not say that a friend's body is no longer material or no longer his body simply because, for example, he gains or loses ten pounds—or even fifty!

Moreover, as many early church fathers pointed out (see Chapter 4), if necessary it would be no problem for an omnipotent God to bring all of the exact particles of one's body together again at the resurrection. Certainly He who created every particle in the universe could reconstitute the relatively few particles (by comparison) in a human body. The God who created the world out of *nothing* is surely able to fashion a resurrection body out of *something*. But, as already noted, this is not necessary, for the resurrection body does not need the same particles in order to be the same body.

Also, in the light of modern science, it is unnecessary to believe that God will reconstitute the exact particles one had in his pre-resurrection body. The physical body before death remains physical, even though the exact physical molecules in it change every seven years or so. So, the resurrection body can be just as material as our present bodies and still have new molecules (particles) in it.

Finally, unlike our bodies, Jesus' body did not undergo corruption while in the tomb. Quoting the psalmist, Peter said emphatically of Jesus, "he was not abandoned to the grave, nor did his body see decay" (Acts 2:31 NIV). Paul adds by contrast that the prophet could not have spoken about David since "his body decayed" (Acts 13:36, 37 NIV). In Jesus' case most, if not all, of the material particles in His pre-resurrection body were available for His resurrection body.[21]

Does Resurrection Restore the Physical Body?

Paul said, "Foods for the stomach and the stomach for foods—but God will destroy both it and them both" (1 Cor. 6:13 NKJV). On this basis some argue that "the resurrection body will not have the anatomy or physiology of the earthly body . . . ."[22] However, this inference is unjustified for a number of reasons.

A careful study of the context reveals that when Paul says God will destroy both food and the stomach he is referring to the *process* of death, not to the *nature* of the resurrection body. He refers to the process of death as the agent by which "God will destroy both it and them."

Also, as already noted, while the resurrection body may not have the necessity to eat, it does have the ability to eat. Eating in heaven will be a joy without being a need.

Furthermore, Jesus ate at least four times in His resurrection body (Luke 24:30, 42; John 21:12; Acts 1:4). His resurrected body was capable of assimilating physical food.

"Flesh and Blood" Cannot Enter God's Kingdom

Paul said "flesh and blood cannot inherit the kingdom of God . . ." (1 Cor. 15:50 NKJV). As early as the second century, Irenaeus noted that this passage was misused by heretics in support of their "very great error."[23] To conclude from this phrase that the resurrection body will not be a body of physical flesh is without scriptural justification.

First, the very next phrase omitted from the above quotation indicates clearly that Paul is speaking not of flesh as such but of *corruptible* flesh. For he adds, *"nor does the perishable inherit the imperishable"* (1 Cor. 15:50 NIV, emphasis mine). Paul is not affirming that the resurrection body will not have flesh, but that it will not have *perishable* flesh.

Second, Jesus said emphatically that His resurrection body had flesh. He declared: "Look at my hands and my feet. It is I myself! Touch me and see; a ghost does not have *flesh and bones,* as you see I have" (Luke 24:39 NIV, emphasis mine).

Peter directly said that the resurrection body would be the same body of *flesh* that went into the tomb and never saw corruption (Acts 2:31). Paul also affirmed this truth in a parallel passage (Acts 13:35). And John implies that it is against Christ to deny that He remains "in the *flesh*" even after His resurrection (1 John 4:2; 2 John 7, emphasis mine).

Third, the orthodox view cannot be avoided by claiming that Jesus' resurrection body had flesh and bones but not material flesh and blood. For if it had flesh and bones, then it was a literal, material body, whether or not it had blood. Flesh and bones are stressed, not blood, probably because they are more visually obvious signs of tangibility than is blood.

Fourth, the phrase "flesh and blood" in this context apparently means *mortal* flesh and blood, that is, a mere human being. This is supported by parallel uses in the New Testament. When Jesus said to Peter, "Flesh and blood has not revealed this to you" (Matt. 16:17 NKJV), He could not have been referring to the mere substance of the body as such, which obviously could not reveal anything, especially that He was the Son of God. Rather, as Schep concludes, "the only correct and natural interpretation [of 1 Cor. 15:50] seems to be that *man, as he now is, a frail, earth-bound, perishable creature,* cannot have a place in God's glorious, heavenly kingdom."[24]

The noted biblical scholar Joachim Jeremias observes that a misunderstanding of this text "has played a disastrous role in the New Testament theology of the last sixty years until the present day." After careful exegesis of the passage, he concludes that "the sentence 'flesh and blood cannot inherit the kingdom of God' does not speak of the resurrection of the dead but rather of the change of the living at the Parousia [Christ's coming]."[25]

Resurrection Is Different from Resuscitation

Some also argue that Jesus' body was not material because His resurrection was more than a resuscitation of a physical corpse. It was a transformation. But this is insufficient grounds to deny the physical nature of the resurrection body for two reasons.

Jesus' resurrection was more than a resuscitation, but it was not less than one. Resuscitated corpses die again, but Jesus' resurrection body was immortal. He conquered death (Heb. 2:14; 1 Cor. 15:54–55), whereas merely resuscitated bodies will eventually be conquered by death. For example, Jesus raised Lazarus from the dead (John 11), but Lazarus eventually died again. Jesus was the first to be raised in an immortal body, one that will never die again (1 Cor. 15:20). However, simply because Jesus was the first to be raised in an immortal body does not mean it was an immaterial body. It was more than a reanimation of a material corpse, but it was not less than that.

Immortal Doesn't Equal Invisible

Also, it does not follow that because Jesus' resurrection body could not die that, therefore, it could not be seen. What is immortal is not necessarily invisible. The recreated physical universe will last forever in its recreated state (Rev. 21:1–4), and yet it will be visible. Here again, the resurrection body differs from resuscitation, not because it is immaterial, but because it is immortal (1 Cor. 15:42, 53).

Jesus Appeared in a "Different Form"

Some propose that after the resurrection "we cannot rule out the possibility that the visible form of Jesus had altered in some mysterious way, delaying recognition of him." They suggest that "the expression 'he appeared in another form' in the Markan appendix (Mark 16:12) encapsulates this."[26] However, this conclusion is unnecessary for several reasons.

First, there are serious questions about the authenticity of this text. Mark 16: 9–20 is not found in some of the oldest and best manuscripts and other ancient witnesses of the biblical text. Many scholars who reconstruct the original texts from the existing manuscripts believe that the older manuscript copies are more reliable, since they are closer to the original manuscripts.[27]

Second, even granting its authenticity, the event of which it is a summary (see Luke 24:13–32) says simply "they were kept from recognizing him" (Luke 24:16 NIV). This makes it clear that the miraculous element was not in Jesus' body but *in the eyes of the disciples* (see Luke 24:16, 31). Recognition of Jesus was kept from them until their eyes were opened.

Third, sound interpretive principles forbid basing a significant Christological doctrine on obscure and/or ambiguous passages.

Fourth, whatever "another form" means, it certainly does

not mean a form other than His real physical, material body. On this very occasion Jesus ate physical food (Luke 24:30), an ability He gave in this chapter of Luke as a proof that He was "flesh and bones" and not an immaterial "spirit" (vv. 38–43).

Jesus Was Raised "In the Spirit" (1 Peter 3:18)

According to Peter, Jesus was "put to death in the flesh, but made alive in the spirit" (KJV). Some have used this to prove that the resurrection body was not flesh but was "spirit" or immaterial. This interpretation, however, is neither necessary nor consistent with the context of this passage and the rest of Scripture.

To begin with, the passage can be translated "He was put to death in the body but made alive by the [Holy] Spirit" (NIV). The passage is translated with this same understanding by the New King James Version and others.

Furthermore, the parallel between death and being made alive normally refers to the resurrection of the body in the New Testament. For example, Paul declared that "Christ died and returned to life . . ." (Rom. 14:9 NIV) and "He was crucified in weakness, yet he lives by God's power" (2 Cor. 13:4 NIV).

In addition, the context refers to the event as "the resurrection of Jesus Christ" (1 Peter 3:21). But this is understood everywhere in the New Testament as a physical bodily resurrection (see Chapters 3, 8).

Even if "spirit" refers to Jesus' human spirit (not to the Holy Spirit), it cannot mean He had no resurrection body. Otherwise, the reference to His "body" (flesh) before the resurrection would mean He had no human spirit then. The terms are not mutually exclusive. It seems better to take "flesh" in this context as a reference to His whole condition of humiliation before the resurrection and "spirit" to refer to His unlimited power and imperishable life after the resurrection.[28]

We Will Be Like Angels in the Resurrection

Jesus said that in the resurrection we "will be like the angels" (Matt. 22:30 NIV). But angels have no physical bodies; they are spirits (see Heb. 1:14). So some argue that we will have no physical bodies in the resurrection. This conclusion, however, is a clear misinterpretation of the passage.

The context is not talking about the nature of the resurrection body, but whether or not there will be marriage in heaven. The question Jesus' statement answered was: "At the resurrection, whose wife will she be of the seven [husbands she had], since all of them were married to her?" (Matt. 22:28 NIV). Jesus' reply was that, like among the angels, there will be no marriage in heaven. The woman will not be married to any of these seven husbands in heaven. Jesus said nothing here about having immaterial bodies in heaven. Such a conclusion is totally outside the context of this passage.

When Jesus said "at the resurrection . . . they will be like the angels in heaven," He obviously meant like angels in that they "will neither marry nor be given in marriage" (Matt. 22:30 NIV). He did not say they would be like angels in that they would have no physical bodies. Rather, they would be like angels in that they would *not marry*.

Does "Life-Giving Spirit" Mean Immaterial?

According to 1 Corinthians 15:45 Christ was made a "life-giving spirit" after His resurrection. Some use this passage to prove that Jesus had no physical resurrection body. But this does not follow for reasons similar to those just given to the previous argument.

The phrase "life-giving spirit" does not speak of the *nature* of the resurrection body but of the divine *origin* of the resurrection body. Jesus' physical body came back to life only by the power of God (see Rom. 1:4). Paul is speaking about its spiritual *source,* not its physical *substance* as a material body.

If "spirit" describes the nature of Christ's resurrection body, then Adam (with whom He is contrasted) must not have had a soul, since he is described as "of the dust of the earth" (1 Cor. 15:47 NIV). But the Bible says clearly that Adam was "a living being [soul]" (Gen. 2:7 NIV).

Also, Christ's resurrection body is called a "spiritual body" (1 Cor. 15:44 NIV) which, as we have seen, is the same word used by Paul to describe material food and a literal rock (1 Cor. 10:4).

Moreover, this "spirit" is called a "body" *soma* which always means a physical body when referring to an individual human being.[29]

In summation, the resurrection body is called "spiritual" and "life-giving spirit" because its source is the spiritual realm, not because its substance is immaterial. Christ's supernatural resurrection body is "from heaven," as Adam's natural body was "of the earth" (1 Cor. 15:47 NIV). But just as the one from "earth" also has an immaterial soul, even so the One from "heaven" also has a material body.

Christ's Immortal, Material Body

In short, there is no scientific, biblical, or theological reason to forsake the historic evangelical view that Jesus was raised immortal in the same observable, material body he possessed before His death. It possessed numerical identity, materiality, and was an event in real history. Despite its immortality, it did not possess immateriality. When present it was as visible and tangible as any other object in the space-time world. As the great biblical scholar Joachim Jeremias put it: "look at the transfiguration of the Lord on the mountain of transfiguration, then you will have the answer to the question how we shall imagine the event of the resurrection."[30]

By no stretch of the imagination did Jesus' pre-resurrection body transform into an immaterial one at this point. Rather, His material body was manifested in its glory. His resurrection body will do the same.

All the arguments used to show that Jesus was raised in a numerically different, invisible, immaterial body fall far short of the mark. To be sure, the resurrection body was imperishable and immortal, but the contention that it was invisible and immaterial is unfounded.

8

Evidence for the Physical Resurrection

As we have seen (in Chapter 7), the theory that the resurrection body is immaterial rests on unfounded speculative inferences. By contrast, the physical, material view of the resurrection body is based on sound logic and direct evidence, especially in the twelve post-resurrection appearances of Christ. Combined with the empty tomb, these appearances provide overwhelming testimony to Christ's victory in our space and time world. They demonstrate that the resurrection body possessed materiality, numerical identity, and historicity, just as orthodox Christians have confessed since the first century. In this chapter we will study these appearances in chronological order, examining them for the various types of evidence of the physical resurrection presented in each.

The Appearance to Mary Magdalene
(John 20:10–18)

It is an unmistakable sign of the authenticity of the Gospel record that in a male-dominated culture, the risen Jesus appeared first to a woman. Anyone faking the record would surely have had Jesus appear first to a more prominent male disciple, such as, Peter. Instead, Jesus' first post-resurrection appearance was to Mary Magdalene. During this appearance there were several unmistakable proofs of the visibility, materiality, and identity of the resurrection body.

First, she *saw* Christ with her natural eyes. The text says, "she turned around and saw Jesus standing there . . ." (John 20:14 NKJV). The word "saw" *(theoreo)* is a normal word for seeing with the naked eye. It is used many times for seeing human beings in their physical bodies (see Mark 3:11; 5:15; Acts 3:16) and even of seeing Jesus in His pre-resurrection body (see Matt. 27:55; John 6:19).

Second, Mary also *heard* Jesus say, "Woman, why are you weeping? Whom are you seeking?" (John 20:15 NKJV). Then again, she heard Jesus say "Mary" and she recognized his voice (v. 16). Of course, hearing alone is not a sufficient evidence of materiality. God is immaterial, and yet His voice was heard in John 12:28. Nevertheless, physical hearing connected with physical seeing *is* significant supportive evidence of the material nature of what was seen and heard. Mary's familiarity with Jesus' voice is evidence of the identity of the resurrected Christ.

Third, Mary also *touched* Christ's resurrection body. Jesus replied, "Do not cling to me, for I have not yet ascended to my Father" (John 20:17 NKJV). The word "cling" *(aptomai)* is a normal word for the physical touching of a material body. It also is used of physical touching of other human bodies (see Matt. 8:3; 9:29) and of Christ's pre-resurrection body (see Mark 6:56; Luke 6:19). The context indicates that Mary was grasping on to him so as not to lose him again. In a parallel experience the women "clasped his feet" (Matt. 28:9 NIV).

Fourth, Mary also went to the tomb and saw that the stone had been removed from the entrance. So she ran to Peter and announced that the body was gone (John 20:2). This would imply that she saw the *empty tomb*. The parallel account in Matthew informs us that the angels said to her, "Come, see the place where the Lord lay" (Matt. 28:6 NKJV). Later, Peter and John also went into the tomb. John "bent over and looked in at the strips of linen lying there" and Peter "went into the tomb. He saw the strips of linen lying there, as well as the *burial cloth* that had been around Jesus' head" (Matt.

28:5–7 NIV). But seeing the same physical body that once lay there is proof of the numerical identity of the pre- and post-resurrection body.

In this one account Jesus was seen, heard, and touched. In addition, Mary witnessed both the empty tomb and Jesus' grave clothes. All the evidence for an unmistakable identity of the same visible, material body that was raised immortal is right here in this first appearance.

Jesus' Appearance to Mary Magdalene and the Other Women (Matt. 28:1–10)

Jesus not only appeared to Mary Magdalene but also to the other women with her (Matt. 28:1–10), including Mary the mother of James and Salome (Mark 16:1). During this appearance there were four evidences presented that Jesus rose in the same visible, material body in which He was crucified.

The women *saw* Jesus. They were told by the angel at the empty tomb, "He has risen from the dead and is going ahead of you into Galilee. There you will *see* him." And as they hurried away from the tomb, "suddenly Jesus met them. 'Greetings,' he said." (Matt. 28:9 NIV). They received visual confirmation of His physical resurrection.

When the women saw Jesus, "they came to him, *clasped his feet* and worshipped him" (emphasis mine). That is, they not only saw his physical body but they felt it as well. Spirit entities cannot be sensed with any of the five senses. The fact that the women actually handled Jesus' physical body is a convincing proof of the material nature of the resurrection body.

The women also *heard*[1] Jesus speak. After giving greetings (v. 9), Jesus said to them, "Do not be afraid. Go and tell my brethren to go to Galilee, and there they will see me" (v. 10 NKJV). Thus the women saw, touched, and heard Jesus with their physical senses, a three-fold confirmation of the physical nature of His resurrection body.

In addition to all this, the women saw the *empty tomb* where that same resurrected body once lay. The angel said to them at the tomb, "He is not here; for He is risen, as He said.

Come, *see* the place where the Lord lay" (v. 6 NKJV). The same "He" who had been dead is now alive, demonstrated by the fact that the same body that once lay there is now alive forever more. So in both the case of Mary Magdalene and the other women, all four evidences of the visible, human resurrection of the numerically identical body were present. They saw the empty tomb where his physical body once lay and they saw, heard and touched that same body after it came out of the tomb.

Jesus' Appearance to Peter (1 Cor. 15:5; compare John 20:3–9)

In 1 Corinthians 15:5 (NKJV), it says Jesus "was seen of Cephas (Peter)." There is no narration of this event, but the text says he was *seen* and implies that he was *heard* as well. Certainly Peter was not speechless. Jesus definitely spoke with Peter in a later appearance when He asked Peter to feed His sheep (John 21:15–17). Mark confirms that Peter (and the disciples) would "*see* him, as He said to you" (Mark 16:7 NKJV, emphasis mine). Peter, of course, saw the *empty tomb* and the grave clothes just before this appearance (John 20:6–7). So Peter experienced at least three of the evidences of the physical resurrection; he saw and heard Jesus, and he observed the empty tomb and grave clothes. These are definite evidences that the body that rose is the same visible, material body He had before the resurrection.

Jesus' Appearance to Two Disciples on the Way to Emmaus (Luke 24:13–35)

During this appearance there were three evidences of the physical resurrection presented. The two disciples not only saw and heard Jesus, but they also ate with Jesus. Combined, they provide clear proof of the material, historical nature of the resurrection.

There were two disciples, one of whom was named Cleopas

(Luke 24:18). As they were walking toward Emmaus, "Jesus himself came up and walked along with them" (v. 16 NIV). Although at first they did not recognize who He was, they nevertheless clearly *saw* Him. When they finally realized who it was, the text says "he disappeared out of their *sight*" (v. 31 NIV, emphasis mine). Jesus' resurrection body was as visible as any other material object.

They also *heard* Jesus with their physical ears (vv. 17, 19, 25–26). In fact, Jesus carried on a lengthy conversation with them. For "beginning at Moses and all the Prophets, he expounded to them in all the Scriptures the things concerning himself" (v. 27 NKJV). Of course, they were not the only ones Jesus taught after the resurrection. Luke informs us elsewhere that "He appeared to them [the apostles] over a period of forty days and spoke about the kingdom of God" (Acts 1:3 NIV). During these times he "gave many convincing proofs that he was alive" (Acts 1:3 NIV).

One further convincing proof of Jesus' physical resurrection was that he *ate* with the two Emmaus disciples. Luke says, "as He sat at the table with them, that He took bread, blessed and broke it, and gave it to them" (Luke 24:30 NKJV). Although the text does not say specifically that Jesus also ate, it is implied by being "at table with them." Later in the same chapter it explicitly states that He ate with the Ten Apostles (v. 43). Luke in two other places states that Jesus did eat with the disciples (Acts 1:4; 10:41). During Jesus' third appearance, the eyewitnesses saw him, heard him, and ate with him over a period of one evening. It is difficult to imagine how Jesus could have done anything more to demonstrate the tangible, material nature of His resurrection body.

Jesus' Appearance to the Ten Apostles
(Luke 24:36–49; John 20:19–23)

When Jesus appeared to the Ten Apostles (Thomas absent), He was seen, heard, touched, and they saw Him eat fish. All four major evidences of the visible, physical nature of the resurrection body were present on this occasion.

First of all, "while they were still talking about this, Jesus himself stood among them and said to them, 'Peace be with you.'" In fact, Jesus carried on a conversation with them about how "everything must be fulfilled that is written about me in the Law of Moses, the Prophets and the Psalms" (Luke 24:44 NIV). Jesus was *heard* by the disciples.

Second, the disciples also *saw* Jesus on this occasion. In fact, they thought at first that He was a "spirit" (v. 7). But Jesus "*showed* them his hands and his feet" (emphasis mine). So they clearly saw Him as well as heard Him. In the parallel account, John records that "the disciples were overjoyed when they *saw* the Lord" (John 20:20 NIV, emphasis mine; see v. 25).

Third, it may be inferred from the fact that they were at first unconvinced of His materiality, that when Jesus presented His wounds to them, they *touched* Him as well. In fact, Jesus clearly said to them, "*Touch* me and see; a ghost does not have flesh and bones, as you see I have" (Luke 24:39 NIV, emphasis mine). The use of "I" and "me" in connection with His physical resurrection body indicates He is claiming to be numerically identical with His pre-resurrection body. Jesus also "showed them his hands and feet," confirming to His disciples that the body they touched was a literal body of "flesh and bones."

Fourth, on this occasion Jesus actually *ate* physical food. In order to convince the disciples that He had resurrected in a literal, physical body, Jesus said, "Do you have anything to eat?" In response, "they gave him a piece of broiled fish, and he took it and ate it in their presence" (v. 43 NIV). What makes this passage such a powerful proof is that Jesus offered His ability to eat physical food as a proof of the material nature of His body of flesh and bones. Jesus literally exhausted the ways in which He could prove the corporeal, material nature of His resurrection body. Thus, if Jesus' resurrection body was not really the same material body of flesh and bones in which He had died, then He must have been a deceiver.

Jesus' Appearance to the Eleven Apostles (John 20:24–31)

Thomas was not present when Jesus appeared to the Ten Apostles (John 20:24). Even after his fellow apostles reported who they had seen, Thomas refused to believe unless he could see and handle Christ for himself. A week later his wish was granted (v. 26). When Jesus appeared to Thomas, he got to see, hear, and touch the resurrected Lord.

Thomas *saw* the Lord. "A week later his disciples were in the house again, and Thomas was with them. Though the doors were locked, Jesus came and stood among them and said, 'Peace be with you!' " (v. 26 NIV). Jesus was clearly visible to Thomas, and Jesus later said to him, "you have *seen* me" (v. 29 NIV, emphasis mine).

Thomas also *heard* the Lord. In fact, he heard the Lord say, "Put your finger here; see my hands. Reach out your hand and put it into my side. Stop doubting and believe" (v. 27 NIV). To this unquestionably convincing display of physical evidence, Thomas replied, "My Lord and my God!" (v. 28 NIV).

It can be inferred from this that Thomas also *touched* the Lord. Certainly this is what Thomas said he wanted to do (v. 25), and this is precisely what Jesus asked him to do (v. 27). The text only says Thomas saw and believed (v. 29), but it is natural to infer that he also touched Jesus. Jesus was touched on at least two other occasions (vv. 9, 17). Thomas encountered a visible, material resurrection body with his natural senses.

Whether Thomas touched Christ or not, he certainly saw His *crucifixion wounds* (vv. 27–29). And the fact that Jesus still had these physical wounds from His crucifixion is an unmistakable proof that He was resurrected in the very same material body in which He was crucified. This was the second time that Jesus "shewed them his hands and feet" (Luke 24:40 KJV). What greater proof could there be that the resurrection body is the same body of flesh that was crucified and then glorified?

Jesus' Appearance to the Seven Apostles (John 21)

John records Jesus' appearance to the seven disciples who went fishing in Galilee. During this appearance the disciples saw Jesus, heard Him, and ate breakfast with Him, thus proving again the visible, material nature of His resurrection body, as well as its real activity in space and time.

They *saw* Jesus, for the Bible says that "Jesus *appeared* again to his disciples by the Sea of Tiberias" (John 21:1 NIV, emphasis mine). Early in the morning they saw Him standing on the shore (v. 4). After He talked and ate with them, the text says "this was now the third time Jesus *appeared* to his disciples after he was raised from the dead" (v. 14 NIV, emphasis mine).

The disciples also *heard* Jesus speak on this occasion (vv. 5–6, 10, 12). In fact, Jesus carried on an extended conversation with Peter in which Jesus asked Peter three times whether he loved Jesus (vv. 15–17). Since Peter had denied Jesus three times, not only did Peter hear Jesus speak, but Jesus' words no doubt rang in his ears. Jesus also told Peter how he would die (vv. 18–19).

Jesus also *ate* with the disciples during this appearance. He asked them, "Friends, haven't you any fish?" (v. 5 NIV). After telling them how to catch some (v. 6), Jesus requested them to "Bring some of the fish you have just caught" (v. 10 NIV). Then He said to the disciples, "Come and have breakfast" (v. 12 NIV). As they did, "Jesus came, took the bread and gave it to them, and did the same with the fish" (v. 14 NIV). Although the text does not explicitly state that Jesus ate, nevertheless, as host of the meal it would have been strange for Him not to have partaken with them. So in addition to seeing and hearing Jesus, He evidenced the material nature of His resurrection by eating physical food.

Jesus' Appearance to All the Apostles at the "Great Commission" (Matt. 28:16–20; Mark 16:14–18)

The next appearance of Christ was when He gave them what we now call the Great Commission (Matt. 28; 16–20).

This time, as Jesus commissioned them to disciple all nations, He was both seen and clearly heard by all the apostles.

The text says that the disciples went to Galilee, where Jesus had told them to go (v. 16). And "when they *saw* him, they worshiped him" (v. 17 NIV, emphasis mine). Mark adds, "Jesus *appeared* to the Eleven as they were eating" (Mark 16:14 NIV, emphasis added).

However, it was not simply *what* they saw, but what they *heard* that left a lasting impression on them. Jesus said, "All authority has been given to Me in heaven and earth. Go therefore and make disciples of all the nations, baptizing them in the name of the Father and of the Son and of the Holy Spirit . . ." (Matt. 28:18–19 NKJV). The fact that this small band shortly became the world's greatest missionary society is ample testimony to how powerfully what the apostles *heard* Jesus speak on this occasion was impressed upon them.

Jesus' Appearance to Five Hundred Disciples (1 Cor. 15:6)

There is no narration of this appearance. It is simply noted by Paul in 1 Corinthians 15:6 where he says, "After that, he *appeared* to more than five hundred of the brothers at the same time, most of whom are still alive" (NIV, emphasis mine).

Since Jesus was *seen* on this occasion and since He left such a lasting impression on them, it can be assumed that they also *heard* Him speak as well. Why else would Paul imply their readiness to testify on behalf of the resurrection, saying in essence, "most of them are still alive. So if you do not believe me, then just go and ask them."

Despite its brevity, this one verse is a powerful testimony to the bodily resurrection of Christ. It has the ring of truth about it. Paul is writing in A.D. 55, only twenty-two years after the resurrection (A.D. 33). Most of these eye witnesses were still alive. Paul challenged his readers to check out what he was saying with this multitude of witnesses who saw and probably heard Christ after His resurrection.

Jesus' Appearance to James (1 Cor. 15:7)

Jesus' brothers were unbelievers before his resurrection. The Gospel of John informs us that "even his own brothers did not believe in him" (John 7:5 NIV). But after His resurrection, both James and Jude, the half brothers of Jesus, became believers (Mark 6:3). However, the Scriptures say explicitly that Jesus "*appeared* to James . . ." (1 Cor. 15:7 NIV, emphasis mine). No doubt Jesus also *spoke* to James. James then became a pillar of the early church and played a prominent part in the first church council (Acts 15:13).

James also wrote one of the books of the New Testament, in which he spoke of "the crown of life" (James 1:12 NKJV) and of the "Lord's coming" (5:8 NKJV) made possible only through the resurrection of Christ (2 Tim. 1:10). Whatever James saw or heard during this resurrection appearance of Christ not only converted him, but also helped make him into a prominent figure in the apostolic church.

Jesus' Appearance to All the Apostles before the Ascension (Acts 1:4–8)

Jesus' last appearance before His ascension was again to all the apostles. During this time they saw Him, heard Him, and ate with Him. These three lines of evidence are confirmation of the literal, material nature of His resurrection body.

Jesus was *seen* by His apostles on this occasion. Luke says, "after his suffering, he *showed* himself to these men and gave many convincing proofs that he was alive" (Acts 1:3 NIV, emphasis mine). He adds, Jesus "*appeared* to them over a period of forty days . . ." (emphasis mine). The text adds that it was "on one [such] occasion" (v. 4 NIV) that Jesus made His last appearance to them.

The apostles also *heard* Jesus, since on this occasion He "*spoke* about the kingdom of God" (v. 3 NIV, emphasis mine). During this specific appearance, Jesus commanded them: "Do not leave Jerusalem, but wait for the gift my

Father promised, which you have heard me speak about" (v. 4, emphasis mine). It was not only a familiar voice, but a familiar teaching, that confirmed to the apostles that it was the very same Jesus speaking to them after the resurrection as before.

Luke also says in this passage that Jesus *ate* with the disciples, as He had done on many occasions. This last appearance before the ascension was "one occasion, while he was eating with them . . ." (v. 4 NIV). This is the fourth recorded instance of Jesus eating after the resurrection. It was apparently something He did rather often, since even the short summary of His ministry by Peter in Acts 10 declares that the apostles "ate and drank with him after he rose from the dead" (v. 41 NIV). Surely, both the intimate fellowship and the physical ability to eat food was more than sufficient proof that Jesus was appearing to them in the same, visible, tangible, material body He possessed before His resurrection.

Jesus' Appearance to Paul after the Ascension (1 Cor. 15:8; Acts 9:1-9)

Jesus also appeared to Paul. In fact, this was Jesus' "last" appearance (1 Cor. 15:8). It is important to note that this appearance was not a vision. This is clear from several considerations. (1) Visions do not have physical manifestations connected with them, such as light. (2) Paul lists this "appearance" as the "last" one right along with the other physical appearances of Christ to the apostles and others in this very chapter. (3) Seeing the resurrected Christ was a condition for being an apostle (Acts 1:22). Paul claimed to be an apostle, saying, "Am I not an apostle? Have I not seen Jesus our Lord?" (1 Cor. 9:1 NIV). (4) The resurrection appearances, including Paul's, are never once called "visions" anywhere in the Gospels or the Epistles (see Chapter 7). They are real physical appearances. During the appearance to Paul, Jesus was both seen and heard, which is indicative of a real physical appearance, not a mere vision.

As for the actual appearance to Paul, Christ was both seen and heard with the physical senses of those present. The physical manifestation of the resurrected Jesus to Paul was both heard and seen by the apostle. In 1 Corinthians 15 Paul said Jesus "*appeared* to me also . . ." (v. 8 NIV, emphasis mine). In the detailed account of it in Acts 26, Paul said "I *saw* a light from heaven . . ." (v. 13 NIV, emphasis mine). That Paul is referring to a physical light is clear from the fact that it was so bright that it blinded his physical eyes (Acts 22:6, 8). Futhermore, Paul not only saw the light, but he also saw Jesus. Referring to this event, he wrote: "Am I not an apostle? Have I not *seen* Jesus our Lord?" (1 Cor. 9:1 NIV, emphasis mine).

Paul also *heard* the voice of Jesus speaking distinctly to him "in Aramaic" (Acts 26:14 NIV). The physical voice Paul heard said, "Saul, Saul, why do you persecute me?" (Acts 9:4 NIV). Paul carried on a conversation with Jesus (vv. 5–6) and was obedient to His command to go into the city of Damascus (v. 6). Paul's miraculous conversion, his tireless efforts for Christ, and his strong emphasis on the physical resurrection of Christ (see Rom. 4:25; 10:9; 1 Cor. 15) all show what an indelible impression the physical resurrection made upon him.

Not only did Paul see the light and hear the voice, but those who were with him did as well (Acts 22:8). This shows that the experience was not private to Paul. It was not purely subjective. It had an objective referent. It happened "out there" in the real physical world, not merely in the world of his private spiritual experience. Anyone who had been there also could have seen and heard the physical manifestation.

The Physical Nature of the Resurrection

The total evidence for the physical, material nature of the resurrection body is overwhelming. The twelve appearances can be summarized in the following chart:

THE TWELVE APPEARANCES OF CHRIST

Persons	*Saw*	*Heard*	*Touched*	*Other Evidence*
Mary	X	X	X	Empty tomb
Mary & Women	X	X	X	Empty tomb
Peter	X	X*		Empty tomb, grave clothes
(John)				(Empty tomb, grave clothes)
Two Disciples	X	X		Ate with Him
Ten Apostles	X	X	X**	Death wounds, Ate with Him
Eleven Apostles	X	X	X**	Death wounds
Seven Apostles	X	X		Ate with Him
All Apostles	X	X		Ate with Him
Five Hundred Brethren	X	X*		
James	X	X*		
All Apostles	X	X		
Paul	X	X		

*Implied   **Offered to be touched

During these twelve recorded appearances Jesus appeared to more than five hundred people over a forty-day period of time (Acts 1:3). On all twelve occasions Jesus was seen and probably heard. Four times he offered Himself to be touched. He was definitely touched twice. Jesus revealed His crucifixion scars on two occasions. There were four times the empty tomb was seen and twice the empty grave clothes were viewed. On another four occasions Jesus ate food.

The sum total of this evidence is overwhelming confirmation that Jesus rose and lived in the same visible, material body he possessed before His resurrection.

9

Lessons to Be Learned

Those who do not know the past are condemned to repeat its errors. Knowing even the immediate past can be helpful in avoiding pitfalls in the present. In this regard many lessons can be gleaned from the "battle for the Bible." Both it and the battle for the resurrection have some strong similarities. Each involves an important doctrine. In both instances evangelicals affirmed their belief in a doctrine, while pouring new meaning into their doctrinal statements. Also, both involved a "spiritualizing" or de-historicizing of a basic doctrine. And, in both cases, those who departed from the orthodox position, nevertheless insisted on claiming the orthodoxy of their unbiblical views.

Lessons in Forming Doctrinal Statements

It is increasingly obvious that the wording of a doctrinal statement is exceedingly important. In formulating a doctrinal statement "an ounce of prevention is worth a pound of cure." Carefully wording doctrinal confessions avoids many difficulties. Two things are noteworthy in this regard.

Doctrinal Statements Cannot Be Too Explicit
While a doctrinal statement the size of the dictionary is undoubtedly too long, brief, one-page statements are probably

too short. (Of course, the strength of a doctrinal statement is more important than the length of its statements.) The doctrines should not only be stated clearly, concisely, and correctly, but also comprehensively.

The need for precise and comprehensive statements has been clearly demonstrated in the "battle for the Bible." Those institutions whose doctrinal statements spoke only of the "inspiration" of the Bible were particularly vulnerable to doctrinal drifting, since "inspiration" could be taken to mean anything from inspiring poetry, like Shakespeare, to the divinely authoritative and inerrant truths of Scripture. As the writings of Jack Rogers of Fuller Seminary showed, even the word "infallible" became a "weasel word." Rogers redefined it to mean unerring in intention only, but not necessarily without any mistakes in its statements.[1]

The word "inerrancy" or its equivalent ("without error") became a necessity. It was more precise, clear, and exclusive enough that it frightened away most people who did not really believe in it.[2] Of course, "inerrancy" means inerrancy of *affirmation* of fact, not just inerrancy of *intention*. All sincere people have inerrant intentions, even when they are wrong.

Jack Rogers and the other faculty members at Fuller Seminary believe in a Bible with the inerrant function of saving (2 Tim. 3:15), but many believe that there are factual misstatements in the Bible. Many Southern Baptist professors also deny inerrancy. Dr. Russell H. Dilday, president of Southwestern Baptist Seminary, moved down this same path when he claimed that "the Bible's infallibility as an authority is based on its purpose and function as a book of eternal truths."[3] This is substantially the same as Jack Rogers's view of a *functional* errorlessness of Scripture.

The former Dean of Trinity Evangelical Divinity School, Kenneth Kantzer, was misled by Jack Roger's equivocal use of the concepts of truth and error. Kantzer mistakenly reported in *Christianity Today* (August 1981) that Rogers had adopted an inerrantist position at the Toronto conference. All Rogers had done was to affirm his long-held view that the Bible never failed to accomplish its saving purposes. While affirming the Bible's unerring *purpose*, Rogers never changed his view that the Bible may have mistaken *propositions* (statements) in it.

The point that was missed in this premature enthusiasm about Jack Roger's view was that he believed the Bible was always without error in its *intention* or function of saving, but not necessarily without error in all of its *affirmation* of fact.[4] Like a generally good map that gets one to his destination and yet has some minor mistakes, Rogers believes that the Bible is without error in its function, but not necessarily in all its facts.

Explicit Statements on the Resurrection

Similar mistakes are now being made over the phrases "bodily resurrection" and "physical resurrection." Professor Murray Harris of Trinity Evangelical Divinity School confesses belief in both (see Chapter 6), but denies that Jesus' resurrection body was a material body of flesh and bones. Many consider Harris' view orthodox, including "Dr. Kenneth Kantzer, director of Trinity's Ph.D. program, [who] issued the final report of the [school] Senate's findings, which recommended the granting of tenure to Harris . . . ."[5] This approval of Harris' view was given in spite of the fact that the report quotes Harris as saying "the Bible teaches a believer's resurrection body is not the 'same substantial body as we had at death.' "[6] But, as we have seen, it is at the heart of the orthodox view to confess that Jesus was raised in the same physical body in which he died.

Explicit, Not Ambiguous

Furthermore, it is premature to pronounce a view *orthodox* until some important ambiguities are clarified concerning what is meant by "bodily resurrection." It could refer to the orthodox belief that the resurrection body was the *same* physical body that died but is now alive forevermore. Or, "bodily resurrection" could be used to refer to the resurrection of a *different* body—namely, an immaterial one—rather than to the resurrection of the one that died. This is not an orthodox belief (see Chapter 6). In this same sense, the phrase "physical resurrection" could mean no more than that the body placed in the tomb was a physical, material body but say nothing about the nature of the body that came out of the tomb. That is, the phrase "physical resurrection" may or may not imply that the body coming out of the tomb via resurrection was the same physical, material body that was placed there.

In brief, it is possible to confess belief in the "physical resurrection" of Christ and still be unorthodox. But when the unorthodox are willing to resort to this level of semantical evasion, the words of Irenaeus are relevant:

> Error, indeed, is never set forth in its naked deformity, lest, being thus exposed, it should at once be detected. But it is craftily decked out in an attractive dress, so as by its outward form, to make it appear to the inexperienced . . . more true than truth itself (*Against Heresies* 1.2).

The ambiguity over the meaning of "physical resurrection" is precisely the point at issue in the current evangelical battle for the resurrection—namely, Was Jesus resurrected in the same physical, material body He had before He died? What is at issue is not simply the resurrection *of* the physical body but the resurrection *in* that same physical body that died. Nor is it a resurrection in an "immaterial physical" body, which is a contradiction in terms. On these points many evangelical doctrinal statements at present are woefully deficient. This is understandable, since the advent of new controversy often requires a more refined use of terminology.

Denials as Well as Affirmations Are Needed

Most current doctrinal statements have only affirmations, that is, "I believe—." This is a significant problem. Often denials are more clear than affirmations. That is, "I *don't* believe—." This is no doubt why many of the Ten Commandments are stated negatively. After all, "Thou shalt be sexually faithful to thy wife" lacks a little of the punch of "Thou shalt not commit adultery." Certainly an affirmation and negation taken together make a much more definitive statement. John 1:3 gives us a good example. Jesus' role as creator is given positively ("through him all things were made") and negatively ("without him nothing was made") (John 1:3 NIV).

A notable exception to the pattern of having only affirmations is the statements on inerrancy produced by the International Council on Biblical Inerrancy (ICBI) in their *Chicago Statement on Biblical Inerrancy* (1978).[7]

> We affirm that the written Word in its entirety is revelation given by God.
> We deny that the Bible is merely a witness to revelation, or only becomes revelation in encounter, or depends on the responses of men for its validity (Article III).

From the affirmation alone, someone could rationalize a neo-orthodox view of Scripture by claiming that the Bible is the written Word of God in the sense that it is an accurate *record* of that revelation, but not that the Bible is the *revelation* of God itself. The denial clearly excludes such a possibility. Hence, the denial is even more clear than the affirmation alone.

Applying this insight to the present battle for the resurrection, the problem could be avoided as follows:

> We affirm that Christ rose permanently from the dead in the same physical body in which He died.
> We deny that Christ's resurrection body was by nature immaterial or invisible.

If evangelical schools had a statement like this, then faculty members with unorthodox views on the nature of the resurrection body would not be able to assent to it conscientiously. Unfortunately, the lack of such a statement makes this lamentable situation possible. Schools and churches with less than definitive statements in this regard cannot expect to avoid difficulties in this area.

Lessons in Interpreting Doctrinal Statements

In addition to learning valuable lessons about formulating doctrinal statements, there are equally important lessons to learn about interpreting them. Two such lessons come to mind. They apply equally well to interpreting the Bible, the U.S. Constitution, doctrinal statements, or to any piece of literature.

Meaning Should Be Read Out of, Not Into, a Text

The true meaning of a passage is the author's meaning, not the reader's. Few but the aberrant "deconstructionist" literary critics seriously believe meaning has its source in the reader, not the author. The author put the meaning into the text, and it is the reader's obligation to read that meaning out of the text. Meaning is what the "meaner" (author) meant, not what the "meanee" (reader) would like it to mean. That is, the real meaning is what was meant *by* the author, not what it may mean *to* the reader (if this is different). This is perhaps the most fundamental rule of interpretation.

One of the most able exponents and defenders of this position is Dr. Walter Kaiser, the Dean of Trinity Evangelical Divinity School. He correctly notes that: "No definition of interpretation could be more fundamental than this: *To interpret we must in every case reproduce the sense the Scriptural writer intended for his own words.*"[8]

Let us apply Kaiser's excellent insights in understanding Scripture to interpreting a typical evangelical doctrinal statement, that of the Evangelical Free Church of America. It has two references to resurrection, one to Christ's resurrection and the other to believers'. They read as follows:

> He [Jesus Christ] rose bodily from the dead, ascended into heaven, where, at the right hand of the majesty on high, He now is our High Priest and Advocate" (Article III C).
>
> We believe in the bodily resurrection of all the dead; of the believer to everlasting blessedness and joy with their Lord, and of the unbeliever to judgment and everlasting conscious punishment (Article III L).

It is clear to anyone familiar with the roots of the Free Church and with the formation of its doctrinal statement that "bodily" means a literal, material body. Several things can be noted in this regard. First, this is the normal meaning of the word "body." Second, this is in continuity with the historic evangelical tradition from which the Free Church emerges. Third, this is what was understood by the official Free Church commentary on the doctrinal statement by its former president, Dr. Arnold T. Olson.[9] Olson commented on Article III, saying, "the Christ beyond death was not merely a spirit, a personality, but a resurrected body." And since the context refers to a "dead body" and those who "dwell in dust," it is clear that he is speaking of resurrection in a physical body. Fourth, the current president of the Trinity Evangelical Divinity School, Kenneth Meyer, understands it as referring to "the literal physical resurrection of Jesus Christ."[10] Likewise, the president of the Free Church, Dr. Thomas McDill's understanding of what is orthodox is quoted in the Free Church *Beacon*. He said "the body of Jesus that was placed in the tomb, when it came out of that tomb it was *physical in nature*, but it was enhanced so that it was no longer a mortal body that would die again."[11] Finally, conversations with noted Free Church leaders verifies that it was "beyond question" that the framers of the Free Church doctrinal statement understood bodily resurrection to mean resurrection in the same physical body in which Jesus was crucified.

But if the Free Church framers meant physical body when they said "body," then there should be no question of allowing any subscriber to this statement to sign it and yet hold views that deny the physical, material nature of the resurrection body. Let us state the case as clearly as possible:

1) The true meaning of a statement is what the framers meant.
2) The framers of the Free Church statement on the resurrection meant physical, material body when they said "body."

3) Therefore, the true meaning of this statement is resurrection in a physical, material body.

Look to the Authors for Meaning

As noted interpreter E. D. Hirsch succinctly stated, "The permanent meaning is, and can be, nothing other than the author's meaning." For "As soon as the reader's outlook is permitted to determine what a text means, we have not simply a changing meaning but quite possibly as many meanings as readers."[12] That is, as soon as the meaning of current leaders replaces that of founding fathers, we have destroyed the value of our doctrinal statements.

In this connection, Alice in Wonderland responded well to Humpty Dumpty's contemptuous use of language when he said, "When *I* use a word it means just what I choose it to mean—neither more nor less." Alice appropriately retorted, "The question is . . . whether you *can* make words mean so many different things."[13] Unfortunately this same "Humpty Dumpty" kind of interpretation is being used by evangelical church leaders to deny major orthodox doctrines such as the physical resurrection. If this "Humpty Dumpty" hermeneutic continues, then all the king's horses and all the king's men won't be able to put our churches back together again!

Statements Should Be Modified if Needed, Not Nullified

From time to time doctrinal statements need to be updated. Just as the change in the usage of words demands an occasionally new translation of the Bible, even so doctrinal statements are subject to the same process. A classic case is the King James use of "let" (see 2 Thess. 2:7). In 1611 the word "let" meant to "hinder." Hence, the New King James (and others) correctly retranslate this word as "restrains." If modern translations did not do this, then by leaving the word the same they are responsible for changing the meaning.

Further, in the case of doctrinal statements, sometimes new issues arise that were not foreseen by the framers of the statement. When this happens, the doctrinal statement needs to be reworded to address these issues in accordance with the meaning of the framers. For these two (and other) reasons it is necessary from time to time to modify doctrinal statements, no matter how good they are. However, integrity demands that when we *change* the wording, we do not change the author's meaning. That is to say, we can state an old doctrine in a new way, but we should not read new meaning into an old doctrine.

When Beliefs Change, Statements Should Be Changed

Of course, from time to time the beliefs of a group change. Sometimes this is for the better; often it is for the worse. But whatever the case, new beliefs should be expressed in new doctrinal statements. That is, a group should properly make a new statement, not improperly read new meaning into the old statement. Likewise, when a faculty member holds a view contrary to that which was meant by the framers in their doctrinal statement, then either the doctrinal statement or the faculty member should be changed. This kind of integrity should begin with the faculty member not signing the doctrinal statement with any "mental reservations." That is, he should not sign it on the basis of what it means to him, but on the basis of what the framers meant by it.

If there is any question about what the framers meant by the statement, then the proper authorities of the church or institution are responsible to make the final judgment in the light of the best evidence available as to what the framers held on the matter. Doctrinal statements are not made of putty. They are not wax noses that can be twisted in any direction. And they should not be stretched to accommodate new and creative views that are at odds with the meanings of the doctrinal statements. Sadly, many evangelical institutions are not following their doctrinal commitments, but are stretching them to embrace views their founders would have readily rejected as unorthodox.

Lessons for Seminary Leaders

Eternal vigilance is the price for orthodoxy, as well as for democracy. We constantly must be alert for doctrinal deviations in our churches and schools. In order to accomplish this, several things are necessary.

The Need for Theologically Educated Leadership

We cannot recognize error unless we know the truth. Neither can we detect a good counterfeit unless we are thoroughly trained in the genuine. Since the Bible is the only divinely authoritative writing for faith and practice, we must be completely acquainted with its contents. Bogus currency is getting so sophisticated that government agents can only tell the genuine from the good counterfeits under a microscope. Likewise, erroneous theological views are often so sophisticated that only an expert in the truth can detect what is wrong with them.

What is true of bogus bills is also true of bogus beliefs. They sound so true and look so true that it is hard to tell that they are not true. In fact, the only way to be sure if they are not true is to scrutinize them under the microscope of God's Word. We must measure them by the Truth. Jesus said of the Scriptures, "Thy word is truth" (John 17:17 KJV).

All doctrine must be measured by the truth of divine Scripture. In order to do this we must know not only the content of Scripture but also the form that content takes in biblical doctrine and in systematic theology. In order to do this, there is no substitute for both correct interpreting and consistent thinking. To accomplish this, training in philosophy is a crucial tool for many reasons. First of all, it is training in how to think, an ability that is on the endangered species list. Furthermore, philosophical training enables one to defend the faith (see Phil. 1:7; 1 Peter 3:15). As C. S. Lewis insightfully noted, "Good philosophy must exist, if for no other reason, because bad philosophy needs to be answered."[14] The same applies to bad theology. In fact usually bad theology has some bad philosophy behind it.

Of course, some will quote Paul, who said to the Colossians, "Beware of philosophy" (Col. 2:8). True, but they forget that we cannot beware of it unless we are aware of it. Few people would go to a doctor who never studied sickness. He has to know something about disease in order to know how to treat it and how not to catch it.

Good Philosophy

Training in philosophy is particularly helpful in spotting false philosophies that masquerade in biblical terminology. For example, the tendency to "spiritualize" or allegorize away the literal historical truth of the Bible is an influence of platonic philosophy that has made a marked impact on the Christian Church at least since the time of Origen (see Chapter 6). And the widespread propensity to consider a story mythical or non-historical if it speaks about the miraculous is a result in the modern world of the antisupernatural philosophies of Benedict Spinoza and David Hume (see Chapter 5). And the more recent movements to stress the subjective and personal elements to the neglect of the objective and historical result from the influence of the existential philosophies of Søren Kierkegaard and Martin Hiedegger. Good philosophy specializes in providing the tools of understanding and critique of these philosophies. Someone trained in philosophy can more easily spot their destructive inroads on Christian teaching.

In this connection it is a giant step backward for schools to close their philosophy departments. The philosophers (and systematic theologians, who depend on philosophy) are particularly adept at detecting theological deviations. Philosophical and theological training for ministers and even lay leaders is crucial for the survival of evangelical Christianity.

The Need to Scrutinize Professors' Writings before Hiring

Many professors have published writings. These should be carefully reviewed by qualified people *before* the professor is hired. In this connection I was shocked to learn from several professors at a well-known school that they had not read the published material of a controversial professor *before* they voted to pronounce his view orthodox. This apparently was also true of most of the faculty that confirmed his appointment. In fact, one prominent faculty member told me he voted to approve of this professor's view as orthodox on what he called "hearsay" information, never having read his book. This is inexcusable and accounts for why some professors are able to slip through the system without their unorthodox views ever being detected.

The question as to how professors with questionable or clearly unorthodox views can be accepted on orthodox faculties is a mystery to many. Thirty years on the faculties of several fine evangelical schools suggests to me several reasons why it happens.

First, although the people who examine prospective teachers are often competent, sometimes they do not ask the right questions. For example, a professor can answer yes to whether he believed in the "bodily resurrection" but no to whether he believed Jesus arose in "the same physical, material body in which He died." But if the second question is never asked, then an unorthodox view can go undetected.

Second, the faculty at large often trusts the judgment of their colleagues who question the candidate. Sometimes this works and sometimes it does not. They may know what the professor affirms, but not always what he denies, especially if they do not question him on the point in dispute. Also, they may understand his affirmations but not fathom all their implications.

Third, all too often the views of the professor in question are not fully known by the faculty until *after* he has been hired or given tenure. But an ounce of prevention is worth a pound of cure. One faculty member on the committee that interviewed a prospective professor, whose views were subsequently questioned, admitted to me that he had not read his book expressing these unorthodox views—this in spite of the fact that it had been in print for several years. When this committee member was later presented with citations from the book, he said, "that is not the impression I got from hearing his statements to the committee." Unfortunately, that is the problem. A verbal presentation without careful scrutiny often "puts the best foot forward" and obscures underlying doctrinal problems.

Fourth, the standards for "orthodoxy" used by the faculty or board on the candidate are not always what the framers meant in the doctrinal statement. The readers of a statement do not always take it to mean what the framers meant by it. And when colleagues are asked to pronounce on one of their own, then it is even more difficult, for fraternity tends to redefine the boundaries of "orthodox" by using a different criterion from the one meant by the framers of their doctrinal statement. Perhaps independent doctrinal boards would be less vulnerable to such influences.

Fifth, once someone has already been pronounced orthodox and given tenure, it is a great embarrassment for an institution and denomination to admit that the system failed. Unfortunately, once the horse is out of the barn, it is a lot easier to say, "Well, I think it was time for him to run anyway." We can't undo our mistakes, but we *can* correct them and learn not to repeat them.

Lessons for Church Leaders

Some schools, especially those connected with denominations, often have added a step in their review of faculty. They require Board review before they grant tenure to a faculty member. This is an excellent check and balance and often works well. However, no system is infallible. Indeed, the system is no better than the people who operate it. Hence, the leaders who direct the process ultimately must shoulder the responsibility for its failure. In this context important lessons can be gleaned for church leaders.

Refutation, Not Condemnation, Is the Proper Procedure

Whenever questions are raised by concerned members of a body, answers should be given. Whenever charges are made, replies should be forthcoming. The way to respond to doctrinal charges is by refutation, not condemnation. When legitimate doctrinal questions are raised by anyone in the body, they should be examined, not exterminated. They should be studied, not squelched.

Attempts to avoid a full and free discussion of the questionable views of professors at evangelical schools on crucial doctrines are inexcusable. When a professor puts his views in print, they become subject to free and open scholarly exchange. Failure to engage in such a dialogue, and attempts to keep negative critiques of such views out of print are unscholarly and unhealthy.

Denominational Issues about Orthodoxy Should Be Aired Fully and Freely

The only way to satisfy the demands of an important doctrinal issue is to allow it to be aired fully and freely. The parties raising questions or bringing charges should be allowed to present their case in person. There must be time for a full and free discussion of the doctrinal issue involved. Decisions should not be "signed, sealed and delivered" without any official group providing opportunity for responsible parties to present the needed evidence.

Opportunity should be given to present the case before the proper boards or committees charged with reviewing these matters. Sufficient time should be allowed for discussion.

Members of a group should not be asked simply to "trust the system." A system should only be trusted if it can be monitored. "Trust but verify." If evangelical denominations and institutions are going to preserve their orthodoxy, procedures not allowing full discussion must be courageously resisted. The members of responsible churches and schools trust their treasurers, but they also have an independent source audit the books. While we must trust those we put in office to lead us, we must also monitor them.

The lack of accountability by evangelical leaders has also led to many recent moral embarrassments for the Body of Christ. Doctrinally, we are just as vulnerable. Members should rely on the system only if they can help regulate it. The failure to do this can be fatal to the doctrinal fidelity of our evangelical institutions.

Lessons for the Media

Since these issues are sometimes given national press attention, it is important to reflect on what can be gleaned from these experiences. A number of lessons emerge worth contemplating.

Impugning Motives of Others Is Wrong

It is always a serious thing to say defamatory things about Christian leaders to the media. The Jim Bakker and Jimmy Swaggart cases should have taught us that Nightline is not the clothes line on which to hang evangelical dirty laundry. Simply because Christians should not take their brothers to court on these matters (1 Cor. 6) does not give us the license to slander one another in the press. Christians have no justification for impugning the motives of others in the public eye. The secular media love to print this kind of "garbage." This leads to another lesson to be learned.

The Responsibility of the Christian Media

Unfortunately the Christian media sometimes react with the same recklessness as the secular media. There are several "No-Nos" in this regard. First, sources should be checked carefully before the material is printed. If this procedure were followed, many stories would never get printed. On this very issue of the resurrection, *Christianity Today* recently printed some false accusations they failed to confirm before printing. When this was brought to their attention, their printed apology read, "We apologize that we did not contact Dr. Geisler for comment before publishing this material." There is a lesson in this for all of us:

"Be careful little hands what you write!"

Another case is the famous "Scopes II" trial in Little Rock, Arkansas, at which I was a witness. An otherwise careful scholar, Dr. Langdon Gilkey, wrote based on a report in the *New York Times* that I had testified to my belief in UFOs based on a report in *Reader's Digest*.[15] The truth of the matter is this: (1) This topic was not part of my prepared testimony at all. (2) The subject was brought up by the ACLU lawyers as an attempt to discredit witnesses in favor of teaching creation along with evolution. (3) The actual court record, which they mysteriously refused to type up until *after* the case went to the Supreme Court (June 1987), shows that the reference was to the testimony of scientists reported in *Science Digest* (November 1981), not *Reader's Digest*! I have seen false reporting based on the *New York Times* article in college textbooks, high school texts, and even one logic text.

Second, the media need to be careful of using biased secular sources. They often have a distorted picture of evangelical issues. The above case illustrates the point. *Christianity Today*'s comments were based on a non-Christian news service without checking with the parties involved. As a result the writer of the *Christianity Today* article had to "eat crow" by admitting: "You're right. We goofed. As the person solely responsible for the article . . . I apologize. We plan to publish your letter in the next available issue, and I hope that will correct the misconceptions created by the article. More importantly, this unfortunate experience will prod us into more thoughtful treatment of all our news articles." The editor went on to explain that they had used a national news service without checking the facts out themselves.

Third, allowing personal attacks to be published, including letters to the editor, should be avoided. They just add more heat than light. Disagreement should be principial, not personal. Above all, nothing should be printed casting doubt on the motives of others. We can and must judge the accuracy and value of actions (see 1 Cor. 6:2f.), but only God can rightly judge the heart (see Heb. 4:12). I deliberately refrain from using illustrations at this point to avoid from even the appearance of judging someone else's motives for judging motives.

Fourth, articles by credible writers on these crucial issues should not be turned down. For example, I have had four publications, including *Christianity Today*, turn down articles on the resurrection, all of which had previously published my material. Two other magazines published articles, but censored material due to pressure placed upon them. Some of the publishers were contacted in advance of the article being sent to them. This kind of information manipulation is reprehensible. However good the motives, it gives the appearance of a cover-up.

Spiritual Lessons

There are also many spiritual lessons to be learned in the struggle to preserve the orthodoxy of our institutions. Space only permits mentioning some here. All of them are taught in Scripture. We must "contend for the faith once for all delivered to the saints" (Jude 3 NIV). But the motives of those who do so should not be judged by others. Jesus said, "Do not judge, or you will be judged" (Matt. 7:1 NIV). Only God knows the "thoughts and attitudes of the heart" (Heb. 4:12 NIV).

Further, we should seek to know all the relevant facts before making a judgment on an issue. For "he who answers before listening—that is his folly and his shame" (Prov. 18:13 NIV). We should always "speak the truth in love" (Eph. 4:15 NIV). We should abstain from gossip and slander against others with whom we disagree (Ps. 15:3; 1 Tim. 5:13). And those who are charged with the responsibility to review the orthodoxy of others should take their responsibility seriously. In so doing, we should not allow considerations of brotherly charity to take precedence over doctrinal purity. Many an institution has sacrificed orthodoxy on the altar of fraternity.

10

Drawing the Line

In defining any fundamental doctrine, a line must be drawn somewhere distinguishing an orthodox understanding from an unorthodox understanding of it. In drawing this line several questions should be kept in mind. What is the biblical teaching on the matter? Also, what is the historic orthodox position on the topic? Finally, does denying this orthodox understanding have serious repercussions on the Christian Faith?

Drawing the Line in the Battle for the Bible

When these three criteria are applied to the battle for the Bible, the line of orthodoxy concerning inspiration should be drawn to exclude those who deny inerrancy. Drawing the line at this point can be justified on all three criteria mentioned above.

Inerrancy Is Taught in the Bible

The biblical claim to inspiration entails inerrancy in several ways.[1] (This position has been ably defended by a coalition of evangelical scholars representing the International Council of Biblical Inerrancy in the book *Inerrancy*.[2]) There are many lines of evidence supporting the view that inspiration entails inerrancy.

One is that God cannot err (Heb. 6:18; Titus 1:2), and the Bible is called the Word of God (Matt. 15:6; John 10:35). Therefore, the Bible cannot err (see Chapters 1–3).

Another is that Jesus affirmed the infallible, indestructible, and unerring nature of Scripture (see Matt. 5:17; 22:29; John 10:35), which affirmation is incompatible with any errors. And since Jesus taught with divine authority (see Matt. 7:24–29; 28:18–20), then on His authority the Bible is the inerrant Word of God.

Yet another line of evidence is that the Bible is the product of the Spirit of Truth (2 Tim. 3:16; 1 Cor. 2:13), and the Spirit of Truth cannot err. So it follows necessarily that the Bible cannot err.

And a fourth is that the Scriptures are "God-breathed" (2 Tim. 3:16). But God cannot breathe out error. His word is absolutely true (John 17:17; Rom. 3:4). What "is written" comes from "the mouth of God" (Matt. 4:4, 7, 10). Therefore, the Bible cannot err anymore than God can.

Also, the Bible is a prophetic message (Heb. 1:1; 2 Peter 1:20–21). But a prophet is a mouthpiece of God (2 Sam. 23:2; Isa. 59:21). He is one through whom *God speaks.* Therefore, the Scriptures cannot be mistaken anymore than God can be. So to speak of the Bible as inspired but errant is a contradiction in terms. An inspired error is as impossible as a square circle.

The Doctrine of Inerrancy Is Supported
by Church History

It has been amply documented that inerrancy has been the orthodox position of the Christian Church down through the centuries. Quotations from the major teachers of the church are collected in our book, *How History Views the Bible: Decide for Yourself.*[3] A scholarly discussion expressing this conclusion is found in John Hannah's *Inerrancy and the Church.*[4]

Jack Rogers's contrary position, stated in *The Authority and Interpretation of the Bible,*[5] was decisively critiqued in Dr. John Woodbridge's book *Biblical Authority: A Critique of The*

Roger/McKim Proposal.[6] A careful examination of the evidence reveals that no orthodox teacher of the Church from the first to the nineteenth century denied the inerrancy of Scripture. Indeed, virtually every orthodox church father believed that the Bible was without error. This has been the standard orthodox position down through the years.

The Crucial Consequences of Denying Inerrancy

It is clear that serious doctrinal consequences follow from denying the inerrancy of Scripture.

For example, to deny inerrancy is to attack the *authenticity* of God the Father. Since the Bible is the Word of God (as I have defined it carefully and repeatedly in this book), to charge the Bible with error is to charge God with error.

Additionally, to admit of error in the Scriptures is to attack the *authority* of God the Son. Jesus said the Bible is wholly true (see John 17:17) and without error (see Matt. 5:17; 22:29). To question that the Bible is the Word of God is in the final analysis to question that Jesus is the Son of God.

Also, to claim there are errors in the Bible is to attack the *ministry* of God the Holy Spirit. The Bible is a Spirit-breathed book (2 Tim. 3:16), and the Holy Spirit cannot breathe-out error.

Finally, to deny inerrancy is to undermine the *stability* of the Christian Church. The Church is based upon the foundation of Holy Scripture given by the apostles and prophets (Eph. 2:20). And the psalmist said, "If the foundation is destroyed, then what will the righteous do?" (Ps. 11:3). The Bible is the fundamental from which the other fundamentals come. And if the fundamental of the fundamentals is not fundamental, then what is? Fundamentally nothing!

In brief, all three tests for orthodoxy support the contention that the line should be drawn to include inerrancy as an essential part of the understanding of the inspiration of the Bible. Therefore, those who affirm inspiration but deny inerrancy are not orthodox on that doctrine, however orthodox they may be on other doctrines.

Drawing the Line in the Battle for the Resurrection

Now these same three criteria for orthodoxy are applicable in the current battle for the resurrection. Some evangelicals are now claiming that a view such as Murray Harris's (see Chapter 6), which denies that Jesus rose in the same material body in which He died, is orthodox. They point to his belief in an empty tomb, subsequent "appearances," and personal continuity of the pre- and post-resurrection Christ as indications of its orthodoxy. But these are clearly not enough, as is evidenced by the fact that even cults like the Jehovah's Witnesses, some New Agers, and many Neo-orthodox believe these and yet deny the orthodox doctrine of the resurrection of Christ.

An empty tomb as such does not prove the resurrection any more than a missing body from a morgue proves it was resurrected. Further, mere appearances or "manifestations" as such do not prove a real resurrection any more than the angelic "manifestations" in the Bible proved these angels had resurrected from the dead. And mere *personal* identity is not enough; there must be a *material* identity as well. That is, the resurrection body must be the numerically same material body that was placed in the tomb.

Orthodox and Unorthodox Views of the Resurrection

Orthodox and unorthodox positions on the resurrection can be contrasted in the following way:

RESURRECTION

ORTHODOX VIEW	UNORTHODOX VIEW
Numerical identity	*No numerical identity*
A material body	*An immaterial body*
An event in history	*Not an event in history*

These two views are not complementary, but contradictory. They cannot be combined nor adhered to simultaneously. Only one can be true. And, as has been pointed out, the orthodox view is true and biblical; the unorthodox view is neither.

The Importance of the Orthodox View

What makes a view on the nature of the resurrection body orthodox is not simply that there was an empty tomb or even appearances of the same person, but that the same observable, material body that died came out of the tomb alive. Otherwise, we have no assurance that Christ overcame death, since that which died was the physical body. Hence, to prove the victory of the resurrection over death it is necessary that the very *same* physical, material body that died be raised from the dead. The claim that Jesus' body changed into an invisible, immaterial one amounts to annihilation, not resurrection.

Another way to show that it was the same body is to note the *numerical identity* between the pre- and post-resurrection body of Christ. This does not mean that every particle (or molecule) in the resurrection body must be the same as those in the pre-resurrection body. The body of a seventy-year-old is numerically the same as his body when he was seven years old, yet it does not have the same particles in it. According to modern science, the particular molecules change about every seven years (see Appendix A).

Numerical Identity of the Resurrection Body

Numerical identity means there is only *one* body involved, not two, even though there may be changes in the particles and size of that one body. Size and particles are only accidental to a body, but having matter is of its very substance. If there is not a numerical identity between the pre- and post-resurrection body, then it is not a resurrection into the same body, but rather a reincarnation into another body. Reincarnation of whatever variety is not a Christian teaching.[7]

Materiality of the Resurrection Body

Second, it is crucial to an orthodox understanding of the resurrection body that it is a *material body*. A material body is the kind of body that died. Therefore, in order to be victorious over death, the resurrection must restore the physical body that died. Of course, it did even better; it rendered the restored physical body immortal (see 1 Cor. 15:54) as well as retained its material nature. But a resurrection that fails to restore the same material body that died is a failure.

The Scriptures often stress the material nature of the resurrection body by calling it *flesh,* since flesh is essential to Christ's full humanity. John describes the incarnation of Christ like this: "the Word became *flesh* and dwelt among us" (John 1:14 NKJV). "Becoming flesh," then, was an essential element of His full humanity. In his epistles John goes even further and declares that any spirit who denies "Jesus Christ has come [and remains] in the flesh" is "not from God" (1 John 4:2 NIV). In this passage he uses the perfect tense, meaning, Jesus came in the flesh in the past and remains in the flesh, even though John wrote this well after the resurrection and ascension of Christ.

In the parallel passage in 2 John 7 (NIV) he uses the present tense, declaring that anyone who "does not acknowledge Jesus Christ as coming [and continuing] in the flesh" is teaching false doctrine. The use of the present tense indicates that John believed it was essential to believe Christ continued to be in the flesh after His resurrection. To deny the *flesh* of the resurrected Christ is to deny His full humanity.

Historicity of the Resurrection and Post-Resurrection Appearances

Third, it is essential to the orthodox understanding of the resurrection to note that it was an event *in space-time history.* Jesus was not only crucified "under Pontius Pilate" (an historical marker), but He was "raised on the third day" which is another obvious historical reference. This phrase is repeated in many of the Christian Creeds (see Chapter 4), but its significance is now being obscured and even denied by some scholars (see Chapter 6). The historicity of the resurrection is crucial to orthodoxy. Christ's death occurred in history (Rom. 5:12), so, His victory over death must also be a historical event. And since death is a historical event, then the resurrection must be also. Just as the pre-resurrection body and the dead body are observable, even so a resurrection body is part of the observable, historical world.

Support for the Orthodox View

There are three lines of evidence supporting the orthodox understanding that Jesus rose in the same, material body of flesh in which He lived and died. They follow the same three criteria used to determine the orthodox understanding of the inerrancy of the Bible.

It Is the Biblical Position

As shown in Chapters 3 and 7, there are numerous lines of evidence which demonstrate that Jesus rose in the same literal, material body in which He died. (1) The tomb was empty; the physical body had departed. (2) That same body that had vacated the tomb was later seen and heard by over five hundred witnesses. (3) Some of these witnesses later touched and handled this same physical body now alive. (4) The pre-resurrection scars were still present in the resurrected body. (5) This reanimated body possessed flesh and bones. (6) It could and did eat physical food on several occasions. (7) The Greek word for body *(soma)* used of it (see 1 Cor. 15:44) always means a physical, material body when used of an individual human being. (8) Paul stressed (by the seed analogy) in 1 Corinthians 15:36–37 that the body (seed) that dies is the same one that rises. (9) Indeed, the close connection between death and resurrection in many passages stresses its physical continuity (see 1 Cor. 15:3–5; Rom. 6:3–5; Col. 2:12). (10) The use of the phrase "resurrection out from among *(ek)* the dead" implies the resurrection of a corpse from among the dead bodies in the tomb (see John 5:28; 1 Cor. 15:12). (11) In addition, the fact that Jesus was physically recognizable in His resurrection body supports this conclusion. (12) It is implied by Paul's offer of hope to sorrowing believers that they will be able to recognize their loved ones in heaven (1 Thess. 4:13–18).

Taken as a whole, this mass of evidence makes it unmistakably clear that the Bible teaches the orthodox view that Jesus rose forever in the very same material body in which he had died. Any denial of this is an unorthodox position on the nature of the resurrection body.

It Was Held by the Orthodox Teachers of the Church

A survey of the great Christian creeds (see Chapter 4) reveals that the confession "I believe . . . in the resurrection of the flesh" has been the apostolic position of the Christian Church down through the ages. The use of the term "flesh" clearly meant material flesh, such as Christ had before His resurrection. With the exception of an unorthodox teacher like Origen, there was not a single major church father who denied that Jesus was raised in His same material body of flesh.

Even when alternate expressions were used, such as "physical" or "bodily," they meant a material body. Belief that Christ's resurrection means a resurrection in the same tangible, material body of flesh in which he was crucified is the orthodox position of the Christian Church.

The Articles of the Church of England (A.D. 1562) emphatically declare,

> Christ did in truth *rise* again from death, and *took again his body, with flesh and bones,* and all things appertaining to the perfection of Man's nature; wherewith he ascended into Heaven, and there sitteth, until he return to judge all Men at the last day.[8]

This could scarcely be more explicit. Christ arose in the exact same body of "flesh and bones" in which He had lived and died. And it is this same body "wherewith" He ascended into heaven.

Likewise, the great Westminster Confession (A.D. 1647) also affirms the historic belief in the physical nature of His resurrection body (Article VII, 4), confessing that He

> was crucified, and died; was buried, and remained under the power of death, *yet saw no corruption.* On the third day he

arose from the dead, *with the same body in which he suffered; with which he ascended into heaven,* and there sitteth at the right hand of his Father . . . .[9]

Here again the language is beyond question: The resurrection body was the "same" physical body Jesus had before His death. In fact, that body "saw no corruption," and that same body "ascended into heaven."

Consequences of Denying the Orthodox View

The denial of this biblical view of the resurrection has serious doctrinal consequences. Another test for the right to call a doctrinal understanding orthodox is that a denial of it has serious consequences for the Christian faith. We have seen (in Chapter 2) many disastrous consequences of denying the material nature of the resurrection body.

Consequences for Creation

God created the material world and gave human beings material bodies (see Gen. 1:1; 2:7). Sin interrupted this plan and brought death and decay (see Gen. 3; Rom. 5; 8). Unless the resurrection of man restores God's material creation, then sin was successful in thwarting God's plan for creation. After all, if Adam had not sinned but had partaken of the tree of life, he would have lived forever in the material body in which God created him. Hence, unless the resurrection restores God's material creation, as Paul declares it will (Rom. 8:19–23), then it was not successful in accomplishing what would have been if Adam had not sinned.

To put it positively, the resurrection body will be just as material as Adam's body was and would have continued to be, had he eaten of the tree of life. Man came from dust and will return to dust. But if he is not reconstituted again out of the dust, then there will be no restoration of God's original creation. In short, either the resurrection body is material or else God lost the creation to Satan.

Consequences for Salvation

Among other things, salvation brings victory over death. It is by the resurrection that we can say: "Where, O death, is your victory?" (1 Cor. 15:55 NIV). Through His death and resurrection Christ was able to "destroy him who had the power of death, that is, the devil . . ." (Heb. 2:14 NKJV). But it was man in his physical material body that died. Therefore, the only way the resurrection could effectively overcome death was if it was a resurrection of the same physical, material body that had died.

Anything short of the material resurrection of the flesh that died would be no real salvation from death. A denial of the material nature of the resurrection body is a concession that Christ failed in His mission to deliver us from the ravages of death. But the Scriptures declare that Christ "through death . . . destroy[ed] him who had the power of death, that is, the devil . . ." (Heb. 2:14 NKJV). By the power of God, who raised him from the dead" Jesus "has delivered us from the power of darkness . . . through His blood . . ." (Col. 1:13, 14 NKJV). The defeat of death came in real history, and so also the victory of resurrection came in history. Anything less than a material resurrection in actual space and time spells defeat, not victory.

Consequences for Christ's Character

There can be no doubt that by His physical appearances in the same scarred body Jesus left upon his disciples the clear impression that He was raised in the same physical body in which He died. Indeed, Jesus even challenged them to feel his wounds (see John 20:27). He said emphatically, "It is I myself! Touch me and see; a ghost does not have flesh and bones, as you see I have" (Luke 24:39 NIV). But if it was not really the same physical body of flesh in which Jesus was crucified, then it seems impossible to avoid the charge that Jesus deliberately misled His disciples. But such a deceptive act is morally culpable. Hence, a denial that Jesus was resurrected in the same physical body in which He died is tantamount to an assault on the character of Christ.

Consequences for Christian Evidences

The resurrection of Christ is the crowning evidence for the Christian faith. The appearances of Christ in His resurrected body are called many "convincing proofs" (Acts 1:3 NIV). It was the physical evidence of the scars that was used by God to convince doubting Thomas of the reality of the risen Christ and elicited his triumphant confession: "My Lord and my God" (John 20:28 NKJV). The resurrection was used as proof of Christ's messiahship in early apostolic preaching (see Acts 2, 4, 10, 13). In fact, the apostle Paul used it effectively even to the conversion of Greek philosophers on Mars Hill, declaring that God "has given proof of this to all men by raising him from the dead" (Acts 17:31 NIV).

Consequences for Christ's Humanity

The Logos was "made flesh and dwelt among us" (John 1:14 NKJV). It was only by assuming human flesh that He could redeem humanity. "Since the children have partaken of flesh and blood, He Himself likewise shared in the same . . ." (Heb. 2:14 NKJV). He had to be both fully God and fully man in order to be the mediator between God and man (see 1 Tim. 2:5). Denying Christ's full humanity is just as disastrous for our salvation as is denying His deity. This is why John declares that any spirit that denies that "Jesus Christ has come in the flesh" is not of God (see 1 John 4:2; 2 John 7).

Christ's enfleshment was necessary for His full humanity. But it has always been part of orthodox teaching that Christ is both God and man, from the point of His conception on for all eternity to come. Therefore, to deny that Christ was raised in the flesh is to deny the completeness of His continuing humanity. It is to say that He was only fully human until He died, but not after He arose. His continued ministry on our behalf in heaven is dependent on His being fully human (see Heb. 2-10).

Consequences for Christian Immortality

Paul declared that Christ "has . . . brought life and immortality to light through the gospel" (2 Tim. 1:10 NKJV). Because He rose, we will rise. But if he did not rise physically, then neither do we have any hope of doing so. The Christian belief in immortality, unlike the Greek's view, was not merely an immortality of the soul but an immortality of the soul-body unity.[10] In fact, every time the word "immortality" is used of humans in the New Testament, it refers to them in their risen bodies (see 1 Cor. 15:53–54; 2 Tim. 1:10). It is never used, as the Greeks used it, of the immortality of a soul separate from a body.

While the soul consciously survives death without a body (see Luke 23:43; Phil. 1:23; 2 Cor. 5:8; Rev. 6:9), nevertheless, the departed believer is incomplete until he receives his resurrection body at the Second Coming (see 1 Thess. 4:13–18; compare Rev. 20:4, 5). So unless Christ was raised in the same physical human body in which he died, there is no real hope of Christian immortality.

Consequences for Christian Hope

If Christ did not rise in the same body in which He died, then neither will we. He is the "firstfruits" (1 Cor. 15:20). If His body was not the same physically recognizable body He had before His death, then neither will we be able to so recognize our loved ones in heaven. For our bodies will be transformed " . . . so that they will be like his glorious body" (Phil. 3:21 NIV). The whole hope that we will again see our loved ones in the flesh is dashed.

Further, unless we do not rise in our same physical bodies, then Paul's encouragement to the Thessalonians was in vain. For the basis of the hope he offered was that bereaved believers will be reunited with their loved ones at the resurrection of believers, when Christ returns (1 Thess. 4:13–18).

In summation, unless Christ rose in the same physical body in which He died, there is no *proof* that he conquered death. Resurrection in an invisible, immaterial body is unverifiable. (And it is not a resurrection of a dead body anyway, but an annihilation of it.) Neither an empty tomb nor mere appearances or "materializations" are sufficient proof of a physical resurrection. Angels can and have "materialized" (see Gen. 18–19), but this does not prove they were raised from the dead. The only way we can know for sure that Jesus conquered death is if he rose in the same material body in which

He had died. Anything short of this is not only unorthodox, but it spells defeat in His effort to overcome the grave. In brief, if Jesus did not win over death in the same material body that died, then He lost. And if He lost, then we are eternally lost (see 1 Cor. 15:18).

A Response to the Cry for Unity above Orthodoxy

Of course, some will cry "Unity! Unity!" They will insist that drawing a line for orthodoxy will exclude some sincere brothers in Christ. What can be said in response to the plea to put unity above doctrinal purity?

First of all, the doctrine of the resurrection is not a luxury in Christian theology. It is an essential without which there is no Christianity. Augustine's famous statement is applicable here: "In essentials unity; in non-essentials liberty, and in all things charity." The bodily resurrection of Christ is an essential, and, therefore, we must demand unity in affirmation of its orthodoxy.

Second, true unity is not possible apart from unity in the truth. The physical resurrection is one of the great truths of the Christian Faith. Therefore, there is no true doctrinal unity apart from belief that Christ was raised in the same physical body in which He died.

Third, what about those who insist that drawing lines will divide Christians? In response it must be lovingly but firmly maintained that *it is better to be divided by truth than to be united by error.* There is an unhealthy tendency in evangelical Christianity to hide under the banner of Christian charity while sacrificing doctrinal purity. While we must always manifest love toward those with whom we disagree, there is no necessity to sacrifice orthodoxy on the altar of unity. If push comes to shove, it is better to be divided by a true understanding of the resurrection than to be united on a false understanding of it. Otherwise, we will be corrupted by compromise.

Fourth, admittedly, drawing doctrinal lines will make doctrinal divisions. But not everything that divides is divisive. Affirming the deity of Christ divides evangelicals from nonevangelicals. But it does not follow, therefore, that evangelicals are divisive for insisting on it as a test of orthodoxy. The same is true of the virgin birth and the vicarious atonement of Christ. All doctrine divides those who believe it from those who do not. In fact, creeds were written to divide truth from falsehood. The fact that there are people who deny fundamental Christian truths does not thereby make those who affirm them divisive.

Of course, no human doctrinal definition is infallible, but this does not mean that some are not crucial. One thing is certain: The lack of clear doctrinal statements is suicidal. The terms in which they are stated are negotiable, but the truth is not.

Finally, *if* anyone should be called divisive for drawing clear doctrinal lines, then it should be the one who *denies* the orthodox, biblical position, not the one who affirms it. Why, for example, should evangelicals be called divisive for affirming the deity of Christ rather than Jehovah's Witnesses for denying it? Why should Bible-believing Christians be called divisive for affirming the virgin birth of Christ? Why not lay the charge at the door of the liberals who deny it? Likewise, why should anyone who affirms the orthodox view on the resurrection of Christ be called divisive, rather that those who deny it? The time has come to put the shoe on the right foot. If anyone is to be called divisive for their doctrinal beliefs, then it should be those who deny the orthodox doctrines, not those who affirm them.

The Bottom Line

The resurrection of Christ is of fundamental importance to the Christian faith. It was the center of apostolic preaching (see Acts 2, 4, 10, 13, 17) and is the heart of the gospel. Paul defined the gospel as the belief that "Christ died for our sins . . . [and] that he was raised on the third day . . ." (1 Cor. 15:1–3 NIV). Belief in the resurrection is laid down by Paul as a condition for salvation. He told the Romans "that if you confess with your mouth, 'Jesus is Lord' and believe in your heart that God raised him from the dead, you will be saved" (Rom. 10:9; see also 1 Thess. 4:14 NIV).

So important was the bodily resurrection of Christ to Christianity that Paul insisted that if Christ did not rise from the grave, then:

1) Our preaching is useless.
2) Our faith is useless.
3) The apostles are false witnesses.
4) Our faith is vain.
5) We are still in our sins.
6) The dead in Christ are lost.
7) We are the most pitied of all men (1 Cor. 15:14–19).

The doctrine of the physical resurrection of Christ is essential to Christianity. There is no real resurrection unless the same physical, material body of flesh that died is restored to life evermore. Therefore, any denial that Christ arose in this same material body of flesh is unorthodox. Christian teachers and preachers who deny the orthodox position on a major doctrine of the Christian faith such as the resurrection should not be retained as leaders in our orthodox institutions.

We must draw a line somewhere. To have no line of demarcation between a false understanding of a doctrine and a true one is to have no true doctrine at all. A creed or confession that can mean anything, means nothing. Painful as it may be, we must not allow doctrinal dilution in our churches and institutions on any of the great fundamentals of the faith that have once for all been delivered to the saints. And it has always been a fundamental of the Christian faith to confess:

"I BELIEVE . . . IN THE RESURRECTION
OF THE FLESH"

Appendices

APPENDIX A

Does the Resurrection Body Have the Same Particles?

Some defenders of the orthodox view have suggested that the resurrection body will have all the same material particles it had before death. Other orthodox teachers do not. Three views need to be distinguished to help clarify the issue.

ORTHODOX VIEW		UNORTHODOX VIEW
Material Body		*Immaterial Body*
Particle View (Every particle restored)	Substance View (Material body restored)	. . . . (No material restored)

Several things are clear from this summary. First, there is a vast difference between the orthodox and unorthodox views. Both cannot be true. The orthodox position holds a literal, material resurrection body, and the unorthodox view denies this.

Second, the intramural debate within the orthodox camp is of no real consequence. The view that every particle of the resurrection body will be restored is possible but not necessary. An omnipotent God can do anything that is not actually impossible. And with the exception of those possesed by two or more cannibals, it is possible to restore every particle to its original owner at the resurrection, even those particles later eaten by other animals. And the God who created man from dust would have no problem providing new particles where two cannibals shared the same ones.

Third, belief that every particle of the pre-resurrection body must be restored is not necessary to the orthodox view. One gets the same substantial material body he had before without holding that every particle of it will be restored in the resurrection. Just as there is identity and continuity in our material bodies that are continually taking on and giving off particles (molecules), even so the resurrection body can be the same material body without having the same material particles as the pre-resurrection body.

After all, a body is more than dust particles. Otherwise, there is a body under my bed! A living body also involves a structure that forms the particles of dust. This same substantial form survives the gain and loss of particular elements while retaining its material nature.

In conclusion, rejecting the particle view does not thereby argue in favor of the unorthodox view. As we have seen, there is another alternative. The assertion that belief in the material nature of the resurrection body is "crassly materialistic" is unfounded.

APPENDIX B

Resurrection Appearances Were Not Theophanies

What is the difference between a post-resurrection appearance of Christ and a theophany? Before answering this, some definitions are necessary. In the Old Testament God sometimes appeared in human form (see Gen. 18–19; Jude 13). These manifestations are called "theophanies" (literally, a *God appearance*). If the second person of the godhead appeared, then it was a Christophany. There are some important differences between a Christophany (or theophany) and the post-resurrection appearances of Christ.

POST-RESURRECTION APPEARANCE	CHRISTOPHANIES
Its Natural State	Not Its Natural State
A Permanent Bodily Form	A Temporary 'Bodily' Form
Previous Physical Body	No Previous Physical Body
Proof Of Resurrection	Not Proof Of Resurrection

A Christophany was not the natural state of the pre-incarnate Christ. Before his incarnation Christ's natural state was immaterial. For He was God, and God is spirit (John 4:24). When one sees a Christophany, however, he is not seeing a spirit with his natural eyes. Rather, what he is seeing is a "materialization" of this spirit. This "materialization" is not the natural state of God who is Spirit (John 4:24), but only a temporary manifestation in human form. Only at His human conception did Christ permanently take on a material human nature in addition to His divine nature.

A Christophany is not different from an angelic manifestation in the Bible, except that in a Christophany it is God Himself who is manifest in human form. The "materialization" is not the natural state of the being who is appearing, whether it is the uncreated God or a created angel.

Old Testament Christophanies were only temporarily assumed forms for the purpose of communicating with human beings. When Christ became human at His incarnation, He took on a permanent human form. He is God forever (John 1:1), but He became man (John 1:14). The human form Christ had on earth, both before and after His resurrection, is a permanent human form. Hence, when Christ appeared after His resurrection, it was in the same human flesh, now glorified, that He possessed before His death.

Unlike resurrection appearances, theophanies are not appearances of a being who once possessed a physical body and then died. Even in Christ's Old Testament appearances as a theophany, He previously had never possessed a human body. Neither did angels who appeared in visible form have physical bodies at any time before their appearances. Theophanies show no continuity with a previous physical body, whereas, a resurrection appearance does.

Unlike a theophany, the appearances of Christ after His death were a proof of His resurrection. For He reappeared in the same physical body that was placed in the tomb and later vacated it alive. And during His post-resurrection appearances, Christ used His crucifixion wounds, His ability to eat fish and to be touched (see Chapter 3) as proof that He was the same person the disciples knew before His crucifixion. That is, He used all these lines of evidence to convince them that the physical appearance they saw, touched, etc., was one and the same as the physical being once dead, but now alive (see Luke 24:39f.). No matter how visible and tangible a theophany appears to be, its mere appearance is never proof that it is a resurrection of a physical body—since God never had a physical body.

In summation, Christ's resurrection appearances were manifestly different from theophanies in several very significant ways. Unlike theophanies, resurrection appearances involved a permanently assumed physical body offered as proof that, though once dead, it is now alive forevermore. Theophanies have none of these characteristics. They occurred before Christ assumed a physical body, and they were only temporary visible forms with no evidential value to demonstrate a resurrection of a previously possessed physical body.

The difference between a post-resurrection appearance and a theophany is very important. If one denies that Christ arose in the same, physical material body in which He died, then there is no way to know that He rose from the dead. Since a theophany does not prove that a being once dead has now come to life, then reducing resurrection to a theophany amounts to a denial of the resurrection itself.

APPENDIX C

Christ's Deity and Humanity Before and After the Resurrection

		ORTHODOX VIEW	UNORTHODOX VIEW
B E F O R E **R E S U R R E C T I O N**	D I V I N E N A T U R E	Infinite Eternal Invisible	Infinite Eternal Invisible

	H U M A N N A T U R E	Mortal
		Historical
		  Space-time
		  Observable
		Material
		  Flesh and bones
		  3-dimensional
			Mortal
			Historical
			  Space-time
			  Observable
			Material
			  Flesh and bones
			  3-dimensional

A F T E R **R E S U R R E C T I O N**	D I V I N E N A T U R E	Infinite Eternal Invisible	Infinite Eternal Invisible
	H U M A N N A T U R E	Immortal body	Immortal body

		Numerical identity
		Material by nature
		  Flesh and bones
		  3-dimensional
		Historical
		  Space-time
		  Observable
		Physical appearances*
			No numerical identity
			Immaterial by nature
			  Not flesh and bones
			  Not 3-dimensional
			Trans-historical
			  Not in space-time
			  Not observable
			Theophanies

*That is, in the same physical body as before the resurrection.

APPENDIX D

The Jewish View of Resurrection

The Old Testament Jewish view of resurrection is crucial to understanding the New Testament view of resurrection, since the latter grows out of the former. Jesus was Jewish, as were all the other New Testament writers, with the possible exception of Luke (see Col. 4:11, 14). There were, of course "liberal" Jews, like the Sadducees, who said "that there is no resurrection" (Matt 22:23). The Pharisees, however, did confess the resurrection (Acts 23:8), and over half of the New Testament books were written by a former Pharisee (Phil. 4:5), Saul of Tarsus, and his travelling companion, Dr. Luke. It is inconceivable that, with this kind of orthodox Jewish background, the New Testament view of resurrection would reflect anything contrary to its Old Testament Jewish heritage.

The Jewish view of resurrection was one of the restoration to life on earth of the physical corpse placed in the tomb. Jews not only believed that man was created "from the dust" (Gen. 2:7) and would return to dust (Eccles. 12:7), but that at the resurrection man would be reconstituted from the dust. This power to bring the dead back to life is expressed in many passages (see Deut. 32:39; 1 Sam. 2:6; Job 19:25–27; Ps. 49:14–15).

First, according to the inspired New Testament (Acts 2; 13), David predicted the resurrection by claiming that "the Holy One will not see decay" (Ps. 16:10 NIV). Peter said of David's prophecy here that "seeing what was ahead, he spoke of the resurrection of Christ, that he was not abandoned to the grave, nor did his body *(sarx)* see decay" (Acts 2:31). Here again, the belief that the resurrection involved a physical body of "flesh" *(sarx)* is unmistakable.

Second, Jesus believed the Old Testament taught resurrection and cited from it to support His position against the Sadducees who rejected the resurrection. As He told them, "You are mistaken, not knowing the Scriptures nor the power of God" (Matt. 22:29). He also cited from Exodus 3:6, 15, saying, "I am the God of Abraham, the God of Isaac, and the God of Jacob" (Matt. 22:32), adding, "God is not the God of the dead, but of the living."

Third, Isaiah spoke of the resurrection of the dead body when he wrote, "Your dead will live: their bodies will rise. You who dwell in the dust, wake up and shout for joy" (Isa. 26:19 NIV). The reference to their "bodies" arising from the "dust" makes evident the identification with physical resurrection.

179

Fourth, Daniel foretold that "multitudes who sleep in the dust of the earth will awake: some to everlasting life, others to shame and everlasting contempt" (Dan. 12:2 NIV). Here again, the reference to "dust of the earth" clearly supports the idea of a physical resurrection.

Fifth, the intertestamental literature also speaks of a physical resurrection. The book of *Wisdom* promises that "in the time of their visitation" the departed "souls of the righteous will be restored and "they will govern nations and rule people" (3:7, 8). Second Maccabees tells of the courageous Jewish believer who suffered his tongue and hands to be cut off, saying, "I got them from Heaven, and because of his laws I disdain them, and from him I hope to get them back again [at the resurrection]" (7:11). Second (Fourth) Esdras predicts that after the time of the Messiah "the earth shall give up those who are asleep in it, and the dust those who dwell silently in it" (7:32). Death is described here as a time "we shall be kept in rest until those times come when thou [God] wilt renew the creation . . ." (7:75).

Sixth, in the apocalyptic writing of 2 Baruch, God is asked, "In what shape will those live who live in Thy day?" The answer is an unequivocal affirmation of belief in the material resurrection: "For the earth shall then assuredly restore the dead [which it now receives, in order to preserve them]. It shall make no change in their form, but as it has received, so shall it restore them, and as I delivered them to it, so also shall it raise them" (49:1; 50:2).

Seventh, Jesus spoke clearly to the Jews of a two-fold resurrection, one "to life" and another "to be condemned" (John 5:28 NIV). "All those who are in the graves will hear his voice and come out . . . ," an obvious reference to physical bodies coming out of the graves.

Eighth, it is evident that the New Testament Pharisees believed in the physical resurrection of the corpse from the tomb. The very story that the Sadducees, who denied the resurrection (Matt. 22:23), used implies that their opponents, the Pharisees, believed in a material resurrection body (see Acts 23:8). For they conceived of the resurrection body as being so physical that it was meaningful to ask which of the wife's seven earthly husbands the woman would be married to in heaven (Matt. 22:28).

Ninth, Mary and Martha reflect the New Testament Jewish belief in the resurrection when they implied that their brother Lazarus could be raised while his body was still in the tomb. Even

Murray Harris, who rejects the Jewish view of a material resurrection, acknowledges nonetheless that "it was impossible, for example, for Jews to believe that Lazarus, who had been dead for four days, could be raised without the removal of the stone that lay over his burial cave and his emergence from the tomb (John 11:38-44)."[1]

It is abundantly clear from these references that the view of Jesus and the New Testament writers grows out of the Old Testament Jewish concept of a resurrection of the same physical, material body placed in the grave. This is particularly true of Paul, an ex-Pharisee, who wrote much of the New Testament. And their views are based on the inspired Old Testament prophecies about resurrection, it would seem necessary to conclude that the New Testament Christian view of resurrection is the same as the Old Testament Jewish view.

APPENDIX E

When Do Believers Receive Their Resurrection Bodies?

Some who deny the material nature of the resurrection body base their belief in part on 2 Corinthians 5:1–10 where Paul says at death believers receive a "heavenly dwelling," a "house not made with hands" (vv. 1–3 NIV). This they identify with Paul's reference to a "spiritual body" (see 1 Cor. 15:44). On this basis they argue that even though one's physical body is in the grave, nonetheless, he receives his resurrection body at the very moment of death.[1]

This view rests in part on a misinterpretation of 2 Corinthians 5:1–10. Several observations are important here.

First, the passage is clearly referring to death, as all agree. And everyone also acknowledges that upon death the physical body is still in the grave. But the resurrection of the physical body cannot occur while the physical body is still in the grave. If it did, then there would be no continuity between what died (the physical body) and what rose. But Paul declared that "*the body* that is sown is perishable, *it* is raised imperishable." He repeats, "*It* is sown . . . , *it* is raised . . ." (1 Cor. 15:42–43). That is to say, the body that dies is the *very same* one to come back to life.

Further, resurrection is described by Jesus as the time when "all who are in the graves will hear his voice and come out . . ." (John 5:28). So while their bodies are in the grave, they are not being raised, and when they are raised their bodies are no longer in the grave. One cannot have it both ways. Resurrection cannot occur while someone's body is still in the grave.

Second, Paul's writings and the rest of Scripture teach plainly that believers are not resurrected until Christ returns again. Daniel said it will be in "the end time" (see Dan. 12:1–2; compare 11:40). Likewise, Martha expected the resurrection "at the last day" (see John 11:24). In fact, Jesus referred to it as "a time coming" when "all who are in the graves" will come out (see John 5:25, 28). Paul pinpointed it as the time when "the Lord himself will come down from heaven . . . and the dead in Christ will rise first" (1 Thess. 4:16 NIV). He told the Corinthians that "when he [Christ] comes" then "those who belong to him" will be made alive" (1 Cor. 15:22–23 NIV). "Then the end will come" (v. 24). Paul also informed the Philippians that "we eagerly await a Savior . . . who will transform our lowly bodies so that they will be like his glorious body" (Phil. 3:20–21 NIV). John foresaw the end time when the dead believers "came to life and reigned with Christ a thousand years" (Rev. 20:4 NIV). This also places the resurrection of believers at the time Christ returns.

But if believers are not resurrected until Christ returns, they obviously are not resurrected at the time of their death. And if they were resurrected, as some claim, at the time of their death, then they will not be resurrected at the time of the Second Coming. In addressing this difficulty, Murray Harris once held that Paul "altered" his view between the time he wrote 1 Thessalonians 4 and the time he penned 2 Corinthians.[2] This is a denial of the inerrancy of Scripture, since on this view Paul was obviously wrong before he changed his position.[3] More recently, however, Harris has opted for an "oscillation" view, wherein Paul is referring to believers *individually* when he speaks of resurrection at death and to them *corporately* when he talks about resurrection at the Second Coming.

However, it is difficult to see how this new understanding avoids the problem. For if each individual believer receives his body at death before the Second Coming, then all believers as a group cannot receive their bodies at the Second Coming. One fails to see how "oscillation" in this sense is anything other than a contradiction. In a penetrating critique of Harris's view, Joseph Osei-Bonsu says flatly, "Such an interpretation of 2 Cor. 5:1–10 is irreconcilable with the Pauline teaching that the resurrection body is received at the Parousia [Second Coming]."[4]

Third, 2 Corinthians 5, and the rest of Scripture for that matter, refers to the moment after death as one of disembodiment, not reembodiment. In this very passage Paul refers to death as being *"naked"* (v. 3) or *"absent* from the body" (v. 8). If death were the moment of resurrection, then Paul should have said "absent from *this* body." In Philippians he speaks of a desire to *"depart* and be with Christ" (1:23). In Revelation 6:9 those who just left their martyred bodies behind are referred to as *"souls"* in heaven. Hebrews 12:23 speaks of heaven as a place where "the spirits of just men are made perfect." Moses and Elijah appeared on the Mount of Transfiguration without resurrection bodies, since Jesus was the first to get one (see 1 Cor. 15:20). But since their physical bodies were in the graves and they had not yet received their resurrection bodies, they must have been in a disembodied state.

Fourth, why should Paul dread death as a state of being "naked" or "unclothed" (vv. 2–4), if one receives his resurrection body at that moment? Speaking of death as disembodiment ("absent from the body") and as an undesirable experience makes little sense if that is the moment of one's ultimate triumph with a resurrection body (see 5:1, 4; 15:50–58).

Fifth, even if Paul is referring to the resurrection body in 2 Corinthians 5, he need not mean that it is received at death. There are other possible ways to explain Paul's reference to "a building from God" that believers receive after death. None of these interpretations involves the highly problematic notion of an immaterial resurrection body.

According to one interpretation, Paul is referring to the intermediate state between death and resurrection and not at all to a resurrection body.[5] In favor of this, it can be noted that Paul does not use the word "body" *(soma)* which when used of a human being always means a physical body.[6] He simply says that when we leave our earthly body ("tent"), we have a "heavenly house" (v. 2). Further, Paul refers to death without resurrection as a state of nakedness, which is undesirable and in need of being clothed (vv. 3–4). At any rate, there is no reference to an immaterial resurrection body in this passage or in any other passage in Scripture (see Chapter 7).

Another interpretive option is that when Paul says "we have," he may be speaking futuristically of the resurrection, not to the disembodied state between death and resurrection. This understanding is linguistically possible.[7] The Greek word translated "we have" could be a futuristic present, referring to the present prospect of a future event. Furthermore, this interpretation is contextually plausible, since Paul is speaking here of the future (see 4:18; 5:4), when death will be swallowed up by life (see 1 Cor. 15:54). Finally, this view fits with Paul's repeated use of the future resurrection as a present hope for believers (1 Thess. 4:13–18; 2 Cor. 4:12).

The source of the mischievous view of an immaterial resurrection body (which Harris contends will be received at death) is identified by Joachim Jeremias as E. Teichmann who published *Die paulinischen von Vorstellungen von Auferstehung und Gerich* (1896). Jeremias says that "a misunderstanding on this issue has played a disastrous role in the New Testament theology of the last sixty years until the present day."[8]

At the heart of the problem for those who interpret 2 Corinthians 5 as resurrection at death is a monistic anthropology. That is, they fail to recognize that while humans are a *unity* of soul and body, they are not an *identity* of the two. They refuse to acknowledge the biblical truth that there is also a duality in man's psychosomatic nature that enables his soul to survive its dissolution from the body. Once they posit a rigid monistic view of man, in order to avoid the absurdity of believing in annihilation (at death) and re-creation (at the resurrection), they must posit an instantaneous resurrection at death. In brief, their "cure" is worse than the "disease." In fact, it is fatal to the orthodox, biblical view of the resurrection.

APPENDIX F

Did Jesus' Resurrected Body Dematerialize?

There are four possibilities with regard to the nature of the resurrection body: (1) It is essentially immaterial but has the ability to become material; (2) It is essentially material but has the ability to cease to be material on occasion (and then become material again); (3) It is essentially material and does not ever cease to be material. (4) It is essentially material and immaterial at the same time.

The last view is contradictory. The resurrection body cannot be both corporeal and incorporeal, extended in space and not extended in space, three-dimensional and not three-dimensional at the same time. The first view is critiqued throughout this book, especially in Chapter 7. The third view is the orthodox view defended throughout this book, especially in Chapters 3, 4, and 8.

However, some argue that the resurrection body is essentially material but occasionally ceased to be material. That is, Jesus was resurrected in a material body, but it could dematerialize and then rematerialize again. They base this position on the fact that the resurrected Christ could disappear immediately, was able to get inside closed rooms, and left His grave clothes in the tomb when He was resurrected. This conclusion does not follow from these facts, and it has some very serious difficulties.

First of all, as was shown in Chapter 7, none of these factors is really evidence that the resurrection body actually ceased to be material on these occasions. Nowhere does the New Testament actually say that the resurrection body went through any physical object. For example, it does not actually say Jesus walked through a closed door. It simply says "with the doors locked for fear of the Jews, Jesus came and stood among them . . ." (John 20:19 NIV). Even if it is inferred from these passages that the resurrection body can move through material objects, it would not have to cease to be material in order to do so. According to contemporary science, a body is mostly empty space and there is no reason why one body cannot pass through another one if they are properly attuned to each other.

Furthermore, Jesus in His pre-resurrection body did supernatural things such as walk on water. But this was no proof that He ceased to be material in order to do this. Otherwise, He in effect received His immaterial resurrection body before His resurrection. If one has to cease to be material in order to walk on water, then Peter must have lost his material body for the brief moments he walked on water (see Mark 14:28–31).

Second, disappearing immediately, as Jesus did on occasion (see Luke 24:31), is not the same as dematerializing. If it is, then Philip the evangelist ceased to be material before his resurrection when he was suddenly transported by the Spirit to another location (see Acts 8:39). This was a supernatural disappearance of his physical body but not a destruction (and later reconstruction) of it. Philip was visible somewhere but not where he had just been.

Third, the empty grave clothes are not a proof that Jesus ceased to be material in order to be raised. The text does not actually say that He passed through His clothes. Here again, the popular idea that they were a kind of cocoon through which His body passed is merely an inference. All the text says is that He left them behind when He left the tomb (see John 20:6–7). Why would the resurrected Christ want to wear blood-stained grave clothes? They were the symbol of His death, not His triumph over it. Furthermore, leaving them behind without the body in them was a sure sign that the physical body was raised.

Rather than being proof of a body that can cease to be material, the empty grave clothes are evidence to the contrary. The fact that the Jesus' burial head cloth "was not lying with the linen wrappings, but rolled up in a place by itself" (John 20:7 NIV) would seem to indicate a deliberate action by a physical body to fold it up. Though Christ could have supernaturally broken through the wall of the tomb, the angels could have rolled back the stone so He could walk out naturally. Rising through the wall of the tomb before the stone was rolled back would have better betokened an immaterial resurrection body. The Bible does not say this is what Jesus did. As it was, all the evidence points to a material body. So convincing was the evidence of an open grave with empty grave clothes that when John saw this, even though he had not yet seen the risen Christ, he "believed" (v. 8).

Fourth, Jesus is said to have been the first to have a resurrection body (see 1 Cor. 15:23). Some of these supposed evidences of the ability to dematerialize came when people were still in their pre-resurrection bodies (e.g., Peter and Philip). Opponents of a material resurrection body forget that simply because the resurrection body can do *more* than a normal physical body does not mean that it is *less* than a physical body.

Even Jesus on the Mount of Transfiguration was still in His material pre-resurrection body, yet it was a glorious body appearing in an unusual manner (see Matt. 17:1–8). Of course, the transfiguration was not a resurrection, since Jesus had not yet died. And one cannot be resurrected, if he has not died. Nonetheless, a resurrection body is more like a Jesus' physical body that was transfigured than a material body that ceased to be material.

Fifth, if a body ceases to be material and later becomes material again, then it is not the same body. It is an annihilation of one material body followed by a recreation of another. This would mean that Jesus had at least twelve different material bodies—one for each post-resurrection appearance. This is not only contrary to common sense, but it is a denial of the New Testament teaching that He was raised in the *same* physical body in which He died (see Chapters 3, 8).

Summary and Conclusion

Contrary to a rather popular misunderstanding of what Jesus did in His resurrection body, there is no evidence that His material body ever dematerialized. According to both the New Testament (see Acts 1:9–10) and orthodox creeds, Jesus even ascended into heaven in the same physical body in which He died and rose in the presence of the disciples. Jesus had just finished "eating with them" (Acts 1:4 NIV) and while "they were looking intently" on Him, Jesus ascended into the sky and disappeared like a rocket in space (1:11).

In his famous work, *Against Heresies*, the early church Father Irenaeus declared emphatically:

> The Church [believes] in one God, the Father Almighty, Maker of heaven and earth, and the sea, and all things that are in them: and in one Christ Jesus, the Son of God, who became incarnate for our salvation; . and the resurrection from the dead, and ascension into heaven in the *flesh* of the beloved Christ Jesus, our Lord [1]

Likewise, St Augustine spoke most explicitly to the nature of the body in which Jesus ascended into heaven, saying, "It is indubitable that the resurrection of Christ, and His ascension into heaven with the *flesh* in which He rose, is already preached and believed in the whole world"[2] (emphasis mine). Augustine adds that this was the belief of the universal Church:

> The world has come to the belief that the *earthly body* of Christ was received up into heaven. Already both the learned and unlearned have believed in the resurrection of the *flesh* and its ascension to the heavenly places, while only a very few either of the educated or uneducated are still staggered by it[3] (Emphasis mine).

These Articles of the Church of England were adopted in 1562 and revised for the Protestant Episcopal Church in the United States in 1801. They declare that Christ ascended into heaven in the same flesh in which He died and rose again.

> Christ did truly *rise* again from death, and *took again his body, with flesh and bones,* and all things appertaining to the perfection of Man's nature; wherewith he ascended into Heaven, and there sitteth, until he return to judge all Men at the last day[4] (emphasis mine).

So it is both unbiblical and unorthodox to claim that Jesus' resurrection body dematerialized in order to accomplish the things He did after His resurrection. Jesus lives today in the same flesh, now glorified, in which He lived and died while on earth. At this very moment His physical body is at a particular place in the universe which the Bible calls "heaven." And the fact that Jesus is in heaven does not make Him any less human. He still makes intercession for us (Heb. 7:25) and, therefore, must be both fully God and fully human.

APPENDIX G

A Survey on the Resurrection

The following survey was sent to the 1,207 members of the Evangelical Theological Society. This is the largest organization of evangelical scholars in the United States. It represents teachers from every section of the country and from all major evangelical denominations and groups. The survey card read as follows:

Resurrection Survey

Please help us in our survey on the resurrection.
Check the box and return immediately.
1. Do you believe Christ rose from the dead in the same material body of flesh and bones in which He died? Yes_____ No_____
2. Do you believe it is unorthodox to *deny* that Christ rose from the dead in the same material body of flesh and bones in which He died? Yes_____ No_____
Do not sign this survey.

There was a 25 percent response. That is, 304 (of 1,207) answered at least one question as follows:
Question 1. 270 checked Yes and 30 No.
Question 2. 256 checked Yes and 37 No.

This means that 88.82 percent of those who responded to the first question affirm their belief that Christ rose from the dead in the same material body in which He died. Likewise, 11.18 percent of all who responded to this question deny that Christ rose in the same material body in which He died.

Further, 84.21 percent of those who replied to the second question believed it was unorthodox to deny that Christ rose in the same material body of flesh and bones in which He died. And 15.79 percent who replied to the second question believed it was not unorthodox to deny this. Slightly less responded to the second question (290) than to the first one (293). Only 6 (2.59 percent) of the 270 persons who responded Yes to the first question responded No to the second question. Some qualified their answers with comments that did not negate their answer to the question

A Word of Evaluation

There was a very good response to the survey (25 percent). This gives a high degree of validity to the results, showing that it represents the broader evangelical community of scholars.

The results show that an overwhelming number of evangelical scholars (nearly 90 percent) believe that Jesus rose in the same material body of flesh and bones in which He died. This is a strong confirmation of the central thesis of this book.

An overwhelming number of those who believed that Christ rose in the same material body (97.41 percent) also believe that it was unorthodox to deny this. That is, nearly everyone (all but 2.59 percent) who answered Yes to the first question also answered Yes to the second question.

An alarming minority of 11 percent of evangelical scholars did not believe in this cardinal dimension of the orthodox doctrine of the resurrection. This shows a significant degree of non-evangelical influence on evangelicals' beliefs about the resurrection.

Notes

Foreword

1. See J. Danielou, *The Origins of Latin Christianity* (London: Darton, Longman & Todd, 1977), pp. 395–404; and J. Pelikan, *The Christian Tradition* (Chicago: University of Chicago Press, 1978), pp. 47–50.
2. See, for example, the comments on this passage in *The New International Commentary* (Grand Rapids: William B.), p. 71 or in J. A. Schep's *The Nature of the Resurrection Body* (Eerdmans Publ. Co., 1978), pp. 71–72.
3. G. W. Dollar, "*Diamond Jubilee Story of the Evangelical Free Church of America* [book review]," *Bibliotheca Sacra* (October 1960), pp. 367–368.

1 The Battle for the Resurrection

1. For a more complete discussion, see Norman L. Geisler and William E. Nix, *A General Introduction to the Bible: Revised and Expanded* (Chicago: Moody Press, 1986), chapters 3–6.
2. See Harold Lindsell, *The Battle for the Bible* (Grand Rapids: Zondervan, 1976).
3. For a more detailed discussion on the inspiration of Scripture, see Geisler and Nix, *A General Introduction to the Bible*, chapters 1–11.
4. For a defense of the inerrancy of the Bible by a coalition of evangelical scholars, see Norman L. Geisler, ed., *Inerrancy* (Grand Rapids: Zondervan, 1979).
5. Wolfhart Pannenberg, *Jesus—God and Man*, translated by Lewis L. Wilkins and Duane A. Priebe (Philadelphia: Westminster Press, 1968), p. 99.
6. Edward Schillebeeckx, *Interim Report on the Books Jesus & Christ* (New York: Crossroad, 1983), p. 75.
7. *Webster's Ninth New Collegiate Dictionary* (Springfield, Massachusetts: Merriam-Webster, Inc., 1985), p. 164.

8. See Robert Gundry, *Soma in Biblical Theology with Emphasis on Pauline Anthropology* (London: Cambridge University Press, 1976), p. 168.

2 *It Makes a Difference*

1. Some of this material appeared in N. L. Geisler, "The Apologetic Significance of the Resurrection," *Bulletin of the Evangelical Philosophical Society* (Spring, 1988), and in "The Theological Significance of the Resurrection," *Bibliotheca Sacra* (April–June, 1989).
2. William G. T. Shedd, *A History of Christian Doctrine* (Minneapolis: Klock & Klock Christian Publishers, n.d.), vol. 2, p. 403.
3. Murray Harris, *Raised Immortal: Resurrection and Immortality in the New Testament* (Grand Rapids: William B. Eerdmans, 1985), p. 132. Harris adds that "Here 'flesh' refers to the material components, the substance, of the body: the flesh-body as distinct from the soul."
4. This is taken from the doctrinal statement of the Evangelical Free Church of America (Article II, 12). The "Doctrinal Statement of Dallas Theological Seminary" is more explicit: "He arose from the dead in the same body, though glorified, in which He had lived and died, . . ." (Article 6).
5. *Webster's Ninth New Collegiate Dictionary* (Springfield, Massachusetts: Merriam-Webster, Inc., 1985), p. 164.
6. Harris, *Raised Immortal*, p. 119.
7. Ibid.
8. This tendency to "spiritualize," along with its concomitant hermeneutic of allegorizing, has reemerged intermittently in the church since the time of Origen and the Alexandrian influence on Christianity. See Chapter 6.
9. See St. Augustine, *City of God*, Nicene and Post-Nicene Fathers, ed. Philip Schaff (Grand Rapids, Mich.: William B. Eerdmans, 1956), XXII, 5, p. 481.
10. Compare 1 Tim. 4:4 and Rom. 14:14.
11. Gundry, *Soma in Biblical Theology*, p. 182.
12. Gundry, ibid.
13. Harris argues there is no material continuity between the pre- and post-resurrection embodiments of Christ. He insists that the continuity is only personal, not substantial. He says, "The identity between the physical and spiritual bodies can scarcely be material or substantial . . ." *(Raised Immortal*, p. 126; see also pp. 54–56). He adds, "one and the same person finds expression in two successive but different types of bodies. There are two dwellings but only one occupant" (p. 126).
14. Gundry, *Soma in Biblical Theology*, p. 176.
15. Gundry, ibid., p. 182.
16. See *The Oxford Dictionary of the Christian Church*, edited by F. L. Cross, 2nd ed. (Oxford: Oxford University Press, 1974), p. 413.
17. See J. A. Schep, *The Nature of the Resurrection Body*, pp. 71–72. He notes of 1 John 4:2 that the perfect participle *(eleluthota)* means "not only that Jesus Christ came in the fullness of time clothed with flesh, but that thus he is *still present* . . . . He is a Christ who 'is come, who came and who abides in the flesh.'"

Commenting on the parallel passage in 2 John 7, A. T. Robertson notes that it is the "Present middle participle of *erchomai* treating the Incarnation as a continuing fact which the Docetic Gnostics flatly denied." See his *Word Pictures in the New Testament* (Nashville: Broadman Press, 1933), vol. 6, p. 253.

18. Harris denies that Jesus was resurrected in the flesh. See Harris, *Raised Immortal,* pp. 124–126.
19. See Harris, ibid., pp. 53, 124, 126.
20. John Updike, "Seven Stanzas of Easter," *Verse* (New York: Fawcett World Library Great Books, 1965).

3 The Bible on the Resurrection

1. Gundry, *Soma in Biblical Theology,* p. 167.
2. For futher discussion of this point, see Chapter 7.
3. Robertson, *Word Pictures in the New Testament,* vol. 5, p. 310.
4. The word "flesh" *(sarx)* is used of the resurrection body in Acts 2:31, which declares that David (in Ps. 16) "spoke of the resurrection of the Christ, that he was not abandoned to the grave, nor did his flesh *(sarx)* see corruption." It is also used in Luke 24:39 where Jesus said He had "flesh *(sarx)* and bones." It is also used in John 1:14 and 1 John 4:2 (and 2 John 7) of Christ in His continued incarnational state both before and after His resurrection (see Schep, *The Nature of the Resurrection Body,* pp. 67–72).
5. The use of the present tense in Greek here means Christ came and remained in the flesh even while this passage was written, which was after the resurrection.
6. Angels who assumed bodily form also ate food on several occasions in the Old Testament (See Gen. 18:8; 19:3). But they never offered their ability to eat food as evidence that they had been resurrected in a material body. Angels are by nature spirits (See Heb. 1:14). Their appearances in visible form are miraculous. Jesus, however, said emphatically, "Touch Me and see, for a spirit does not have flesh and bones as you see that I have" (Luke 24:39 NASB). In view of these crucial differences, the fact that angels ate cannot be used to prove that their temporarily assumed "bodies" were of the same nature as Christ's resurrection body. Furthermore, there was no claim on the angels' part to have once been in a physical body, nor to be now resurrected in that body, scars and all. The cases are significantly different and so nothing can be inferred validly from this one similarity.
7. See Chapter 4.
8. See William F. Arndt and F. Wilbur Gingrich, *A Greek-English Lexicon of the New Testament* (Cambridge: Cambridge University Press, 1959), pp. 290–291.
9. Gundry, *Soma in Biblical Theology,* p. 176.
10. Harris, *Raised Immortal,* p. 39.
11. Gundry, *Soma in Biblical Theology,* p. 177.
12. Harris, *Raised Immortal,* pp. 126, 124.
13. Gundry, *Soma in Biblical Theology.*
14. Ibid., p. 168.
15. Ibid., p. 168.
16. As to why Paul did not use the word "flesh" *(sarx),* see note 1 above.
17. Gundry, *Soma in Biblical Theology,* p. 169.

4 "I Believe in the Bodily Resurrection"

1. J. A. Schep, *The Nature of the Resurrection Body,* p. 221.
2. Ibid., p. 223.
3. Irenaeus, *Against Heresies* 1.10.1. Translated by Alexander Roberts and James Donaldson in *The Apostolic Fathers of The Ante-Nicene Fathers* (Grand Rapids, Mich.: Wm. B. Eerdmans, reprinted from 1885 ed.), vol. 1, p. 330.
4. Ibid., Chapter 7, vol. 1, p. 532
5. Ibid., Chapter 3, vol. 3, p. 530.
6. Tertullian, *The Prescription Against Heretics,* Chapter XIII in *Ante-Nicene Fathers,* vol. 3, p. 249.
7. Ibid.
8. Justin Martyr, *On the Resurrection, Fragments* in *The Ante-Nicene Fathers,* vol. 1, section 10, p. 298.
9. Ibid., Chapter 2, p. 295.
10. Ibid., Chapter 8, p. 297.
11. Ibid., Chapter 9, p. 298.
12. Ibid.
13. Athenagoras, *The Resurrection of the Dead,* Chapter 3, in *Ante-Nicene Fathers,* vol. 2, p. 150.
14. Cited by Schep, *The Nature of the Resurrection Body,* p. 225.
15. *Two Creeds of Epiphanius: Second Formula* (A.D. 374) in Philip Schaff, *The Creeds of Christendom: With a History and Critical Notes* (Grand Rapids: Baker Book House, 1983), vol. 2, p. 37.
16. Cyril of Jerusalem, *Catechetical Lectures* (Lect. 14, 21) in Philip Schaff, *Nicene and Post-Nicene Fathers of the Christian Church* (Grand Rapids, Mich.: Wm. B. Eerdmans, 1983), vol. 7, p. 99.
17. Ibid., Lecture 18, 22, p. 139.
18. Ibid., Lecture 18, 18, p. 139.
19. St. Augustine, *City of God,* Book 22, 5, in Philip Schaff, ed., *The Nicene Fathers* (Grand Rapids, Mich.: Wm. B. Eerdmans, 1956), vol. 2, p. 482.
20. Ibid., emphasis added.
21. Ibid., 22, 14, p. 495.
22. Ibid., 22, 20, p. 498.
23. Of course, in view of modern science, it is unnecessary to believe, as Augustine did, that the physical resurrection body will have the identical particles of the pre-resurrection body. For even the molecules of the pre-resurrection body change every several years, yet it remains the same physical body (see Appendix A).
24. St. Anselm, *Cur Deus Homo* (Book 2, chap. 3), translated by S. W. Deane in *St. Anselm: The Basic Writings* (La Salle, Ill.: Open Court, 1962), p. 241.
25. Ibid., Book 2, Chapter 11, pp. 255-256.
26. Ibid., Book 2, Chapter 3, p. 242.
27. St. Thomas Aquinas, *Compendium of Theology,* 153, in Thomas Gilby, *St. Thomas Aquinas: Philosophical Texts* (New York: Oxford University Press, 1964), no. 764.
28. St. Thomas Aquinas, *III Summa contra Gentiles,* 79, in Thomas Gilby, *St. Thomas: Theological Texts* (Durham, North Carolina: The Labyrinth Press, 1982), no. 662.

29. St. Thomas Aquinas, *IV Summa contra Gentiles*, 81, in Gilby, *St. Thomas: Theological Texts*, no. 6.
30. Ibid., no. 7.
31. Ibid., no. 10.
32. Ibid., no. 12.
33. Ibid., no. 13.
34. Schaff, *Creeds of Christendom*, vol. 3, p. 98.
35. Ibid., p. 99.
36. Ibid., p. 183.
37. Ibid., pp. 368–369.
38. Ibid., p. 404.
39. Ibid., pp. 433–434.
40. Ibid., p. 489.
41. Ibid., pp. 620–621.
42. Ibid., pp. 731–733.
43. Ibid., p. 748.
44. See ibid., pp. 749f.
45. Schep, ibid., pp. 222, 227.
46. Murray Harris, *Raised Immortal*, p. 132.
47. Ibid., p. 127.
48. Ibid., p. 124.
49. In addition, this new way to deny the unorthodox view claims the resurrection body will be *"without physical instincts"* and *"will not have the anatomy or physiology of the earthly body . . ."* (Harris, *Raised Immortal*, pp. 123, 124, emphasis mine).
50. Harris, *Raised Immortal*, p. 53.
51. Edward Schillebeeckx, *Interim Report*, p. 75.

5 Denials of the Bodily Resurrection

1. See Norman L. Geisler, *Miracles and Modern Thought* (Grand Rapids, Mich.: Zondervan, 1982), Chapter 1.
2. Benedict Spinoza, *Tractatus Theologico-Politicus* in *The Chief Works of Benedict de Spinoza*, translated by R. H. M. Elwes (London: George Bell and Sons, 1883), 1.83, 87, 92.
3. Ibid., p. 92.
4. Ibid., p. 107.
5. David Hume, *An Inquiry Concerning Human Understanding*, edited by C. W. Hendel (New York: Bobbs-Merrill, 1955), 10.1.118.
6. Ibid., pp. 118–123.
7. Ibid., pp. 122–123.
8. Antony Flew, "Miracles," in Paul Edwards, ed., *The Encyclopedia of Philosophy*, vol. 5, p. 347.
9. Douglas E. Lurton, ed., *Thomas Jefferson: The Life and Morals of Jesus of Nazareth* (New York: Wilfred Funk, Inc., 1943), p. 132.
10. Robert Jastrow, *God and the Astronomers* (New York: W. W. Norton & Co., Inc., 1978), p. 15.
11. Ibid., p. 115.
12. Ibid., p. 14.

13. Sir Fred Hoyle and N. C. Wickramasinghe, _Evolution from Space_ (London: Dent & Sons, 1981), pp. 24–26.
14. C. S. Lewis, _Miracles_ (New York: Macmillan, 1947), p. 109.
15. Ibid., p. 108.
16. Rudolf Bultmann, _Kerygma and Myth: A Theological Debate,_ edited by Hans Werner Bartsch, translated by Reginald H. Fuller (London: Billing and Sons, 1954), pp. 38–39.
17. Ibid., pp. 39–40.
18. Gary Habermas, _The Verdict of History: Conclusive Evidence for the Life of Jesus_ (Nashville: Thomas Nelson, 1984).
19. F. F. Bruce, _The New Testament Documents: Are They Reliable?_ (Grand Rapids, Mich.: Wm. B. Eerdmans, 1960).
20. John W. Montgomery, _Christianity and History_ (San Bernardino, Calif.: Here's Life, 1983).
21. See Norman L. Geisler and William E. Nix, _General Introduction to the Bible,_ p. 475.
22. H. S. Reimarus, _Reimarus: Fragments,_ translated by R. S. Fraser (London: SCM, 1971).
23. William L. Craig, _Knowing the Truth About the Resurrection_ (Ann Arbor, Mich.: Servant, 1988), Chapter 2. Professor Craig has written some of the best scholarly material in defense of the literal, material resurrection of Christ. See his massive 677-page tome, _The Historical Argument for the Resurrection of Jesus During the Deist Controversy_ (Lewiston: Edwin Mellen, 1985).
24. Kirsopp Lake, _The Historical Evidence for the Resurrection of Jesus Christ_ (London: William & Norgate, 1907), pp. 247f.
25. Frank Morrison, _Who Moved the Stone?_ (Grand Rapids, Mich.: Zondervan, 1978), pp. 97f.
26. See Josh McDowell, _The Resurrection Factor_ (San Bernardino, Calif.: Here's Life, 1981), pp. 92f.
27. _The Journal of the American Medical Society_ 255:11 (March 21, 1986), p. 1463.
28. David Strauss, _A New Life of Jesus_ (London: Williams and Norgate, 1879), vol. 1, p. 412.
29. Hugh J. Schonfield, _The Passover Plot: New Light on the History of Jesus_ (New York: Bantam Books, 1967).
30. Edwin M. Yamauchi, _Gordon Review_ 10:3 (Summer, 1967), pp. 150f. This was also reprinted in John W. Montgomery, ed., _Christianity for the Tough-Minded_ (Minneapolis: Bethany, 1973), pp. 261–271.
31. See William F. Albright in an interview in _Christianity Today_ (January 18, 1963).
32. John A. T. Robinson, _Redating the New Testament_ (Philadelphia: The Westminster Press, 1976), pp. 352–353.
33. They were condemned at the Council of Alexandria (402), the Council of Constantinople (543), and The Second Council of Constantinople (553). See F. L. Cross, ed., _The Oxford Dictionary of the Christian Church,_ p. 1010.
34. Origen, _Against Celsus_ 4.1.16, in Philip Schaff, _Ante-Nicene Fathers,_ vol. 4, p. 365.
35. Origen, _De Principiis_ 3.6, in Schaff, _Ante-Nicene Fathers,_ p. 347.
36. Ibid., 6.68, p. 604.

37. Ibid.
38. Ibid., 6.7, p. 347.
39. Ibid.
40. Ibid., 7.32, p. 623.
41. Ibid., 3.5, p. 346.
42. Ibid., 7.22, p. 623.
43. Ibid., 6.29, p. 586.
44. Ibid., 5.23, p. 553.
45. Ibid., 5.18, p. 551.
46. Ibid., 5.19, p. 551.
47. J. F. Rutherford, *The Truth Shall Make You Free*, (Brooklyn: Watchtower Bible and Tract Society, 1943) p. 264.
48. Ibid.
49. Samuel Rutherford, *Let God be True* (Brooklyn: Watchtower Bible and Tract Society, 1946), p. 272.
50. Samuel Rutherford, *The Harp of God*, (Brooklyn: Watchtower Bible and Tract Society, 1921) p. 172.
51. J. F. Rutherford, *The Truth Shall Make You Free*, p. 264.
52. Samuel Rutherford, *Let God be True*, p. 122.
53. Rutherford, *The Harp of God*, p. 172.
54. Charles Taze Russell, *Studies in the Scriptures*, (Brooklyn: Watchtower Bible and Tract Society) vol. 2; *The Time is at Hand*, p. 129.
55. Charles Taze Russell, *The Kingdom is at Hand*, (Brooklyn: Watchtower Bible and Tract Society, 1944) p. 259.
56. Russell, *The Time is at Hand*, (Allegheny, Penn.: Tower Publications, 1888) p. 127.
57. Levi H. Dowling, *The Aquarian Gospel of Jesus the Christ* (Santa Monica, Calif.: DeVorss & Co., 1907, 1964). Further references to this book are given in the text.
58. The Aquarian "Jesus" goes on to give his pantheistic message, saying, "What I have done, all men will do; and what I am, all men will be" (v. 30).

6 *Denials of the Bodily Resurrection within the Church*

1. See Edward Schillebeeckx, *Jesus: An Experiment in Christology,* translated by Hubert Hoskins (New York: Seabury Press, 1979). Under ecclesiastical pressure, Schillebeeckx modified some of his positions in the direction of orthodoxy, but he did not change them on the immaterial nature of the resurrection body. See Ted Schoof, ed., *The Schillebeeckx Case* (New York: Paulist Press, 1984), especially pp. 135–158.
2. Edward Schillebeeckx, *Jesus: An Experiment in Christology,* translated by Hubert Hoskins (New York: Seabury Press, 1979), p. 522. All page citations from this book are placed in the text for handy reference.
3. Other Roman Catholic scholars have strongly objected to Schillebeeckx's view of the resurrection. See *Interpreting Jesus* (Ramsey, N. J.: Paulist Press, 1983), pp. 121–123.
4. Emil Brunner, *The Christian Doctrine of Creation and Redemption: Dogmatics,* vol. 2, translated by Olive Wyon (Philadelphia: The Westminster Press, 1952), p. 372.

5. Rudolf Bultmann, *Kerygma and Myth*, pp. 38–39.

6. Ibid., pp. 39–40.

7. Ibid., pp. 40, 42.

8. Ibid., p. 42.

9. Wolfhart Pannenberg, *Jesus—God and Man*, translated by Lewis L. Wilkins and Duane A. Priebe (Philadelphia: Westminster Press, 1968), p. 101. All page citations from this book are placed in the text for handy reference.

10. George Eldon Ladd, *I Believe in the Resurrection of Jesus* (Grand Rapids, Mich.: Eerdmans, 1975). All page citations from this book are placed in the text for handy reference.

11. Ronald Nash, *Christian Faith and Historical Understanding* (Grand Rapids, Mich.: Zondervan, 1984), p. 128.

12. E. L. Glenn Hinson, *Faith of Our Fathers: Jesus Christ* (Wilmington, North Carolina: McGrath Publishing Company, 1977), pp. 59f. All page citations from this book are placed in the text for handy reference.

13. *Raised Immortal* was first published in 1983 in England by Marshall Morgan & Company. It was reprinted without revision by Wm. B. Eerdmans Publishing Company in 1985. Harris has an earlier article touching on the matter titled "Resurrection and Immortality: Eight Theses," *Themelios*, 1:2 (Spring, 1976), pp. 50–55. Here, too, he rejects "substantial or numerical identity" between the pre- and post-resurrection body in favor of "two dwellings but one occupant" (p. 55). He claims that "the New Testament nowhere explicitly refers to 'the resurrection of the body' or 'the resurrection of the flesh'" (p. 51). Rather, at resurrection "the physical body may be said to be *transformed into* the spiritual body or to be *replaced by* the spiritual body" (p. 127).

14. All page citations from Harris's writings in this section will be placed in the text for handy reference.

15. Harris, *Raised Immortal*, p. 58. He calls resurrection "historical" in the unusual sense of an event that is real and objective but not observable with the natural senses. Indeed, he insists that "it was the Resurrection not the Ascension that marked the terminus of Christ's sojourn on earth . . ." (p. 50).

16. Ibid., p. 58. In support of his statement here, Harris quotes people like Reginald Fuller, Emil Brunner, J. Moltmann, and others who call the resurrection "meta-historical" or the like.

17. Harris, *Raised Immortal*, p. 58.

18. Ibid.

19. Murray Harris, *Easter in Durham: Bishop Jenkins and the Resurrection of Jesus* (Exeter: The Paternoster Press, 1985). All page citations from this booklet are placed in the text for handy reference.

20. Murray Harris, "Raised . . . Never to Die Again," *Voices* (Deerfield, Ill.: Trinity Evangelical Divinity School, 1988), 14:2, pp. 12–13. All page citations from this article are placed in the text.

21. Harris, *Raised Immortal*, p. 54.

22. This letter was published in the Evangelical Free Church *Beacon* (July 11, 1988).

23. This letter (dated February 6, 1989) was sent to Pastor Samuel Kostreva III, pastor of an Evangelical Free Church in Lodi, Wisconsin, in response to his question

7 Bodily Resurrection vs. Immaterial Resurrection

1. See Arndt and Gingrich, *A Greek-English Lexicon of the New Testament*, p. 685.
2. Ibid.
3. The manna is also called "bread of God," "bread from heaven," and even "bread of angels" (See John 6:32–33; Ps. 78:25). Again, all of these "spiritual" descriptions are of literal physical food that the Israelites picked off the ground each morning except Saturday (See Ex. 16; Num. 11).
4. Colin Brown, *The New International Dictionary of New Testament Theology* (Grand Rapids, Mich.: Zondervan, 1979), vol. 3, p. 707.
5. See Harris, *Raised Immortal* (Grand Rapids, Mich.: Wm. B. Eerdmans, 1985), pp. 46–47.
6. The usual word for "vision" is *orama*, not *horao* (see Matt. 17:9; Acts 9:10; 16:9). In the New Testament it always refers to seeing something that is essentially invisible, such as God or angels.
7. The Greek aorist passive tense is used here, implying that Jesus took the initiative in appearing to them.
8. See Edwin Hatch and Henry Redpath, *A Concordance to the Septuagint and Other Greek Versions of the Old Testament* (Grand Rapids, Mich.: Baker Book House, 1987), vol. 2, 105–107. For futher references, see *opthe* which is used of ocular vision (Karl H. Rengstorf, *Die Auferstehung Jesu*, 2nd ed. [Witten-Ruhr: Luther-Verlag, 1954], pp. 93ff; and Ronald Sider, "St. Paul's Understanding of the Nature and Significance of the Resurrection in 1 Corinthians XV 1–19" *Novum Testamentum* [April, 1977], vol. 19, fasc. 2, pp. 124–141).
9. When the expression "he let himself be seen" *(ophthe)* is used of God or angels (See Luke 1:11; Acts 7:2), who are invisible realities, then *in that context* it refers to an invisible entity becoming visible. But since the same expression is used of other humans with physical bodies and since Christ is said to have had a body *(soma)*, there is no reason to take the expression to refer to anything but a physical, material body, unless the context demands otherwise.
10. See Harris, *Raised Immortal*, pp. 53–54.
11. Arndt and Gingrich, *A Greek-English Lexicon of the New Testament*, p. 581.
12. Gerhard Friedrich, ed., *The Theological Dictionary of the New Testament*, translated by Geoffrey W. Bromiley (Grand Rapids, Mich.: Wm. B. Eerdmans, 1977), vol. 5, p. 356.
13. Fritz Rienecker, *A Linguistic Key to the Greek New Testament*, translated by Cleon Rogers (Grand Rapids, Mich.: Zondervan, 1976), p. 439.
14. Harris does *not* use this point to support his view (see his *Easter in Durham*, pp. 23–24, and *Raised Immortal*, pp. 61–62), but Pannenberg does (*Jesus—God and Man*, pp. 93–95, 99). However, Harris's view amounts to the same thing. For he argues that the resurrection body was essentially immaterial (*Easter in Durham*, p. 17) and could only be seen with the natural eye if a miracle occurred by which it "materialized." So for all practical purposes, there is little difference in insisting that a miracle of materialization occurred or a miracle of visualization. Both views deny the essential materiality or physicality of the resurrection body. Ironically, both views posit some kind of miracle to do it

15. Pannenberg, *Jesus—God and Man*, p. 93.
16. Friedrich, ed., *Theological Dictionary of the New Testament*, vol. 5, p. 357.
17. "Physical" here means something that is part of the material world that can be experienced through one or more of the five senses without any supernatural aid.
18. Those with Paul heard the "sound" (see Acts 9:7), but they "did not understand the voice" (22:9 NIV). That is, they heard the audible sound but did not understand the meaning of what was said.
19. Since the text does not explicitly say how Jesus got in behind closed doors, any suggestion is only speculation. We do know that angels used their special powers to unlock prison doors to release Peter (see Acts 12:10). The supernatural Christ certainly possessed this same power.
20. Harris, *Raised Immortal*, p. 126.
21. Of course, there may have been some dissolution involved in Jesus' body. Death itself involves some breaking down of organic molecules. In any event there was no *eventual* dissolution, since His resurrection quickly reversed death (see Schep, *The Nature of the Resurrection Body*, p. 139).
22. Harris, *Raised Immortal*, p. 124.
23. Irenaeus, *Against Heresies* 30, 13, in Roberts and Donaldson, eds., *The Ante-Nicene Fathers*, vol. 1, p. 357.
24. Schep, *The Nature of the Resurrection Body*, p. 204.
25. Joachim Jeremias, "'Flesh and Blood Cannot Inherit the Kingdom of God,'" *New Testament Studies II* (1955-56), p. 157.
26. Harris, *Raised Immortal*, p. 56.
27. See Geisler and Nix, *General Introduction to the Bible*, pp. 486–489.
28. Schep, *The Nature of the Resurrection Body*, p. 77.
29. See Gundry, *Soma in Biblical Theology*, p. 168.
30. Jeremias, "'Flesh and Blood Cannot Inherit the Kingdom of God,'" *New Testament Studies II*, p. 157.

8 *Evidence for the Physical Resurrection*

1. The "hearing" of Christ in the resurrection appearances is not to be confused with "hearing" God's "voice" in a vision (see Chapter 7).

9 *Lessons to Be Learned*

1. Jack Rogers, ed., *Biblical Authority* (Waco, Texas: Word Books, 1977), chapter 2; and *The Authority and Interpretation of the Bible: An Historical Approach* (New York: Harper & Row, 1979), pp. 426ff.
2. Clark Pinnock is an exception. In his book *The Scripture Principle* (New York: Harper & Row, 1984), he comes to the ironic conclusion that, in spite of the fact that the Bible contains minor mistakes and factual inaccuracies, the word "inerrancy" should be used to describe it.
3 Russell H. Dilday, *The Doctrine of Biblical Authority* (Nashville: Convention Press, 1982), p. 96.
4. See N. L. Geisler, "The Concept of Truth in the Inerrancy Debate," *Bibliotheca Sacra* (October-December, 1980) for futher discussion on this point.
5 This is taken from the Free Church *Beacon* (November 7, 1988) article head-

lines: "Dr. Murray Harris Cleared of All Allegations Regarding His View on the Resurrection Body of Christ."

6. The quote goes on to say that "the same atoms as are in our body at death need not compose the resurrection body." But this is not the point under dispute. The question is not whether the resurrection body has the same *atoms* as the pre-resurrection body but whether it is, to borrow Harris's own words, "the same substantial *body*." That is, the question is not whether the resurrection body has the same material *particles* but whether it is the same material body (see Appendix A). This Harris denies, and this the Bible and the orthodox creeds affirm (see Chapters 3, 4).

7. See Norman L. Geisler, ed., *Inerrancy* (Grand Rapids, Mich.: Zondervan, 1979), pp. 494–497.

8. Walter Kaiser, "Legitimate Hermeneutics," in Norman L. Geisler, ed., *Inerrancy* (Grand Rapids, Mich.: Zondervan, 1979), p. 118.

9. See A. T. Olson, *This We Believe* (Minneapolis: Free Church Publications, 1965), pp. 206–208, 334–337.

10. Letter from Dr. Kenneth Meyer to me dated December 4, 1987.

11. Thomas McDill, *Beacon* (September 5, 1988).

12. E. D. Hirsch, *Validity in Interpretation* (New Haven: Yale University Press, 1967), p. 213.

13. Lewis Carroll, *Alice's Adventures in Wonderland* and *Through the Looking Glass* (New York: Signet, 1960), p. 186.

14. C. S. Lewis, *The Weight of Glory* (New York: Macmillan, 1945), p. 50.

15. Langdon Gilkey, *Creationism on Trial: Evolution and God at Little Rock* (Minneapolis: Winston, 1985), p. 77.

10 Drawing the Line

1. See Geisler and Nix, *A General Introduction to the Bible* (Chicago: Moody Press, 1986), Chapter 3.

2. Geisler, ed., *Inerrancy* (Grand Rapids, Mich.: Zondervan, 1979).

3. Norman L. Geisler, *How History Views the Bible: Decide for Yourself* (Grand Rapids, Mich.: Zondervan, 1982).

4. John Hannah, *Inerrancy and the Church* (Chicago: Moody Press, 1984).

5. Jack Rogers and Donald K. McKim, *The Authority and Interpretation of the Bible: An Historical Approach* (New York: Harper & Row, 1979).

6. John D. Woodbridge, *Biblical Authority: A Critique of the Rogers/McKim Proposal* (Grand Rapids, Mich.: Zondervan, 1982).

7. See Norman L. Geisler and J. Yutaka Amano, *The Reincarnation Sensation* (Wheaton, Ill.: Tyndale, 1986).

8. Schaff, *The Creeds of Christendom*, p. 489, emphasis added.

9. Ibid., pp. 620–621, emphasis added.

10. See George Elton Ladd, "The Greek Versus the Hebrew View of Man," *Present Truth* (February, 1977), pp. 78–84

Appendix D The Jewish View of Resurrection

1. Harris, *Raised Immortal*, p. 39.

Appendix E When Do Believers Receive Their Resurrection Bodies?

1. Harris, *Raised Immortal*, pp. 44, 100.
2. Murray Harris, "2 Corinthians 5:1-10: Watershed in Paul's Eschatology," *Tyndale Bulletin* (1971), pp. 33, 45.
3. For a critique of this view, see Ben F. Meyer, "Did Paul's View of the Resurrection of the Dead Undergo Development?" *Theological Studies* 47:3 (1986), pp. 363-387; and Andrew T. Lincoln, *Paradise Now and Not Yet* (Cambridge: Cambridge University Press, 1981), pp. 69-66.
4. Joseph Osei-Bonsu, "Does 2 Cor. 5.1-10 Teach the Reception of the Resurrection Body at the Moment of Death?" *Journal for the Study of the New Testament* 28 (October, 1986), p. 81.
5. See K. Hanhart, *The Intermediate State in the New Testament* (Groningen, 1966), p. 173; and R. V. G. Tasker, *The Second Epistle of Paul to the Corinthians* (London, 1958), pp. 77-81.
6. Gundry, *Soma in Biblical Theology*, p. 168.
7. See J. H. Moulton, *Grammar of New Testament Greek* (Edinburgh, 1903), vol. 1, p. 120; and C. F. D. Moule, *An Idiom Book of New Testament Greek*, 2nd ed. (Cambridge: Cambridge University Press, 1959), p. 7.
8. Jeremias, "'Flesh and Blood Cannot Inherit the Kingdom of God,'" *New Testament Studies II*, pp. 157-158.

Appendix F Did Jesus' Resurrected Body Dematerialize?

1. Irenaeus, *Against Heresies*, 1.10.1, in the *Ante-Nicene Fathers*, vol. 1, p. 330, emphasis added.
2. St. Augustine *City of God*, Book 22, 5, in Schaff, ed., *The Nicene Fathers*, vol. 2, p. 482.
3. Ibid.
4. Ibid., p. 489.

Glossary of
Important Terms

Body. The physical organ of interaction with the external world; the outer material dimension of man in contrast with his inner, immaterial aspect, which is called "soul" or "spirit."

Corporeal. From the Latin *corpus*, "body," which means having a physical body.

Death (Physical). The separation of soul and body, the point of departure from this life.

Flesh. The physical, material body, or a person in such a body, as opposed to spirit, which is immaterial (See).

Immaterial. Not material or physical; spiritual by nature.

Incorporeal. Not corporeal; having no physical body.

Material. Composed of matter, visible and tangible, and extended in space.

Physical. From *physis*, "nature," referring to man's material as opposed to his immaterial dimension.

Resurrection. Coming back to life, the reversal of death, the permanent reanimation of a dead body.

Soul. The immaterial aspect of human nature that animates the material body.

Spirit. In this book, used interchangeably with "soul"; the invisible, nonmaterial dimension as opposed to "flesh."

Spiritual. Spirit-like, immaterial, or invisible by nature.

"Spiritual" (Greek: pneumatikon). Dominated or guided by the spirit; having a divine or supernatural source but including material things such as food, rocks (1 Cor. 10:3–4), and people in bodies both before (2:15) and after the resurrection (15:44).

Select Bibliography

Aquinas, Thomas, *Summa contra Gentiles III.*

Athenagoras, *The Resurrection of the Dead,* Chapter 3 in Ante-Nicene Fathers, edited by Philip Schaff. Grand Rapids, Mich.: William B. Eerdmans, 1977.

Augustine, *City of God,* Book XXII.

Boliek, L. E., *The Resurrection of the Flesh.* Grand Rapids, Mich.: William B. Eerdmans, 1962.

Camp, Norman H., *The Resurrection of the Human Body.* Chicago: The Bible Institute Colportage Association, 1937.

Craig, William L., *Knowing the Truth About the Resurrection.* Ann Arbor: Servant, 1988.

Gundry, Robert, *Soma in Biblical Theology With Emphasis on Pauline Anthropology.* Cambridge: Cambridge University Press, 1976.

Habermas, Gary, *The Verdict of History: Conclusive Evidence for the Life of Jesus.* Nashville: Thomas Nelson, 1984.

Irenaeus, *Against Heresies.* In *Ante-Nicene Fathers,* vol. 1.

Jeremias, Joachim, "Flesh and Blood Cannot Inherit the Kingdom of God." In *New Testament Studies* 2 (1955–56).

Landis, Robert W., *The Doctrine of the Resurrection of the Body Asserted and Defended; In Answer to the Exceptions Recently presented by Rev. George Bush.* Philadelphia: Perkins & Purves, 1846.

Lincoln, Andrews, T., *Paradise Now and Not Yet.* Cambridge: Cambridge University Press, 1981.

Martyr, Justin, *On the Resurrection, Fragments.* In *The Ante-Nicene Fathers: The Apostolic Fathers,* vol. 1 sect. X.

McCann, Justin, *The Resurrection of the Body.* New York: Macmillan, 1928.

McDowell, Josh, *The Resurrection Factor.* San Bernardino, Calif.: Here's Life, 1981.

Meyer, Ben F., "Did Paul's View of the Resurrection of the Dead Undergo Development?" In *Theological Studies* 47:3 (September 1986).

Miller, Lawrence William, S. T. M., *The Christian's Resurrection Body: Its Nature and Characteristics.* Grand Rapids, Mich.: Zondervan, 1937.

Montgomery, John W., *History and Christianity.* San Bernardino, Calif.: Here's Life, 1983.

Orr, James, *The Resurrection of Jesus.* New York: Jennings & Graham, 1909.

Osei-Bosnu, "Does 2 Cor. 5.1–10 Teach the Reception of the Resurrection Body at the Moment of Death?" In *Journal for the Study of the New Testament* 28 (October, 1986).

Schep, J. A., *The Nature of the Resurrection Body.* Grand Rapids, Mich.: William B. Eerdmans, 1964.

Sider, Ronald, J., "St. Paul's Understanding of the Nature and Significance of the Resurrection in 1 Corinthians XI 1–19." In *Novum Testamentum* (April, 1977), vol. 19, fasc. 2.

Sider, Ronald, "The Pauline Conception of the Resurrection Body in 1 Corinthians XV. 35–54." In *New Testament Studies* 21 (1975).

Smith, Wilbur, "Resurrection." In *Baker's Dictionary of Theology.* Grand Rapids, Mich.: Baker Book House, 1978.

Tenney, Merrill C., *The Reality of the Resurrection.* New York: Harper & Row, 1963.

Scripture Index

Extra-Biblical References

Topical Index

216